Praise for *Fostering School–Family Relationships in Multicultural Communities*

"This book's insightful approach to bridging diverse cultural perspectives within educational settings truly resonates with my professional experiences, and I believe its research, practical strategies, and thoughtful analysis will significantly contribute to advancing dialogue and practice in school–family partnerships. I look forward to supporting this important work and am excited to see its impact on educators and community leaders."

—**Patricia A. Edwards**, University Distinguished Professor, Michigan State University, College of Education

"If we hope to cultivate meaningful, lasting, trusting family–school relationships, we must reimagine what those relationships can and ought to be and then adjust everything we're doing; the old *five easy strategies* never, ever work. The authors model something more transformative, stepping us through that reimagining process, contextualizing valuable practical strategies in even more valuable expansions of understanding."

—**Paul C. Gorski,** founder, Equity Literacy Institute, and coauthor with Katy Swalwell of *Fix Injustice, Not Kids and Other Principles for Transformative Equity Leadership*

"*Fostering School–Family Relationships in Multicultural Communities* invites parents and educators to ask the questions that often go unasked about children and schools. It challenges readers to center on what really matters for children, suggesting that if we aspire to raise children who care about others and their world, we must revisit current school practices and provide opportunities for children and youth to question, explore their passions, and wrestle with new ideas. This is a book to be not only read, but discussed widely among educators, parents, and anyone else who cares about children, youth, and schools."

—**Catherine Compton-Lilly**, John C. Hungerpiller Professor, University of South Carolina

"This book is an important reminder of how structural and systemic forces are necessary to build and cultivate family–school partnerships and connections. Written as more than a set of recommendations to build individual relationships across difference, this book shows us what can happen when we, collectively and unapologetically, place students front and center in the work of education."

—**H. Richard Milner IV**, Cornelius Vanderbilt Chair of Education, Vanderbilt University, and author, *The Race Card*

MULTICULTURAL EDUCATION SERIES

JAMES A. BANKS, Series Editor

Fostering School-Family Relationships in Multicultural Communities
MATTHEW KNOESTER, MAURA G. ROBINSON, & TOUORIZOU HERVÉ SOMÉ

Affirming Student Ethnic Identities: How Teachers Can Create Welcoming Classrooms
ANDRÉ J. BRANCH

Critical Theory, Methods, and Design in Educational Research
LOIS WEIS & MICHELLE FINE

Critical Ethnic Studies and the Global Pursuit of Justice
JAMES WRIGHT

Let's Talk About DEI: Productive Disagreements About America's Most Polarizing Topics
SHAUN HARPER

Why Historically Black Colleges and Universities Matter: 25 Years of Historical Research for Justice
MARYBETH GASMAN

Hidden in Blackness: Being Black and Being an Immigrant in U.S. Schools and Colleges
CHRYSTAL A. GEORGE MWANGI & ADAURENNAYA C ONYEWUENYI

"To Remain an Indian": Lessons in Democracy from a Century of Native American Education, 2nd Ed.
K. TSIANINA LOMAWAIMA AND TERESA L. MCCARTY

From Foster Care to College: Navigating Educational Challenges and Creating Possibilities
ROYEL M. JOHNSON

Achieving Equal Educational Opportunity for Students of Color: Disrupting Structural Racism—An American Imperative
RICHARD R. VALENCIA

Critical Multicultural Education: Theory and Practice
CHRISTINE E. SLEETER

Race and Media Literacy, Explained (or Why Does the Black Guy Die First?)
FREDERICK W. GOODING, JR.

Whiteness in the Ivory Tower: Why *Don't* We Notice the White Students Sitting Together in the Quad?
NOLAN L. CABRERA

Culturally Sustaining Policymaking in Indigenous Communities: Partnering to Promote Lasting Change
APRILLE J. PHILLIPS

Educating for Equity and Excellence: Enacting Culturally Responsive Teaching
GENEVA GAY

Speculative Pedagogies: Designing Equitable Educational Futures
ANTERO GARCIA & NICOLE MIRRA, EDS.

Seeing Whiteness: The Essential Essays of Robin DiAngelo
ROBIN DIANGELO

Becoming an Antiracist School Leader: Dare to Be Real
PATRICK A. DUFFY

The Hip-Hop Mindset: Success Strategies for Educators and Other Professionals
TOBY S. JENKINS

Education for Liberal Democracy: Using Classroom Discussion to Build Knowledge and Voice
WALTER C. PARKER

Critical Race Theory and Its Critics: Implications for Research and Teaching
FRANCESCA LÓPEZ & CHRISTINE E. SLEETER

Anti-Blackness at School: Creating Affirming Educational Spaces for African American Students
JOI A. SPENCER & KERRI ULLUCCI

Sustaining Disabled Youth: Centering Disability in Asset Pedagogies
FEDERICO R. WAITOLLER & KATHLEEN A. KING THORIUS, EDS.

The Civil Rights Road to Deeper Learning: Five Essentials for Equity
KIA DARLING-HAMMOND & LINDA DARLING-HAMMOND

Reckoning With Racism in Family-School Partnerships: Centering Black Parents' School Engagement
JENNIFER L. MCCARTHY FOUBERT

Teaching Anti-Fascism: A Critical Multicultural Pedagogy for Civic Engagement
MICHAEL VAVRUS

Unsettling Settler-Colonial Education: The Transformational Indigenous Praxis Model
CORNEL PEWEWARDY, ANNA LEES, & ROBIN ZAPE-TAH-HOL-AH MINTHORN, EDS.

Culturally and Socially Responsible Assessment: Theory, Research, and Practice
CATHERINE S. TAYLOR, WITH SUSAN B. NOLEN

LGBTQ Youth and Education: Policies and Practices, 2nd Ed.
CRIS MAYO

For a complete list of series titles, please visit www.tcpress.com/MCE

(continued)

Multicultural Education Series, *continued*

Transforming Multicultural Education Policy and Practice
James A. Banks, Ed.

Critical Race Theory in Education
Gloria Ladson-Billings

Civic Education in the Age of Mass Migration
Angela M. Banks

Creating a Home in Schools
Francisco Rios & A Longoria

Generation Mixed Goes to School
Ralina L. Joseph & Allison Briscoe-Smith

Indian Education for All
John P. Hopkins

Racial Microaggressions
Daniel G. Solórzano & Lindsay Pérez Huber

City Schools and the American Dream 2
Pedro A. Noguera & Esa Syeed

Measuring Race
Robert T. Teranishi et al.

Transformative Ethnic Studies in Schools
Christine E. Sleeter & Miguel Zavala

Why Race and Culture Matter in Schools, 2nd Ed.
Tyrone C. Howard

Just Schools
Ann M. Ishimaru

"We Dare Say Love"
Na'ilah Suad Nasir et al., Eds.

Teaching What *Really* Happened, 2nd Ed.
James W. Loewen

Culturally Responsive Teaching, 3rd Ed.
Geneva Gay

Music, Education, and Diversity
Patricia Shehan Campbell

Reaching and Teaching Students in Poverty, 2nd Ed.
Paul C. Gorski

Deconstructing Race
Jabari Mahiri

Is Everyone Really Equal? 2nd Ed.
Özlem Sensoy & Robin DiAngelo

Transforming Educational Pathways for Chicana/o Students
Dolores Delgado Bernal & Enrique Alemán Jr.

Un-Standardizing Curriculum, 2nd Ed.
Christine E. Sleeter & Judith Flores Carmona

Global Migration, Diversity, and Civic Education
James A. Banks et al., Eds.

Reclaiming the Multicultural Roots of U.S. Curriculum
Wayne Au et al.

We Can't Teach What We Don't Know, 3rd Ed.
Gary R. Howard

Diversity and Education
Michael Vavrus

Mathematics for Equity
Na'ilah Suad Nasir et al., Eds.

Race, Empire, and English Language Teaching
Suhanthie Motha

Black Male(d)
Tyrone C. Howard

Race Frameworks
Zeus Leonardo

Class Rules
Peter W. Cookson Jr.

Achieving Equity for Latino Students
Frances Contreras

Literacy Achievement and Diversity
Kathryn H. Au

Understanding English Language Variation in U.S. Schools
Anne H. Charity Hudley & Christine Mallinson

Latino Children Learning English
Guadalupe Valdés et al.

Asians in the Ivory Tower
Robert T. Teranishi

Diversity and Equity in Science Education
Okhee Lee & Cory A. Buxton

Forbidden Language
Patricia Gándara & Megan Hopkins, Eds.

The Light in Their Eyes, 10th Anniversary Ed.
Sonia Nieto

The Flat World and Education
Linda Darling-Hammond

Educating Citizens in a Multicultural Society, 2nd Ed.
James A. Banks

Culture, Literacy, and Learning
Carol D. Lee

Facing Accountability in Education
Christine E. Sleeter, Ed.

Talkin Black Talk
H. Samy Alim & John Baugh, Eds.

Improving Access to Mathematics
Na'ilah Suad Nasir & Paul Cobb, Eds.

Beyond the Big House
Gloria Ladson-Billings

Improving Multicultural Education
Cherry A. McGee Banks

Transforming the Multicultural Education of Teachers
Michael Vavrus

Learning to Teach for Social Justice
Linda Darling-Hammond et al., Eds.

Learning and Not Learning English
Guadalupe Valdés

Multicultural Education, Transformative Knowledge, and Action
James A. Banks, Ed.

Fostering School–Family Relationships in Multicultural Communities

Matthew Knoester, Maura G. Robinson, and Touorizou Hervé Somé

Series Foreword by James A. Banks

Published by Teachers College Press,® 1234 Amsterdam Avenue,
New York, NY 10027

Front cover design by Holly Grundon / BHG Graphics. Photo by FatCamera / iStock by Getty Images.

Library of Congress Cataloging-in-Publication Data is available at loc.gov

ISBN 978-0-8077-8752-6 (paper)
ISBN 978-0-8077-8753-3 (hardcover)
ISBN 978-0-8077-8331-3 (ebook)

Printed on acid-free paper
Manufactured in the United States of America

Dedicated to the memory of a beloved aunt and teacher,
Patricia A. Knoester (1951–2025)

Contents

Series Foreword

Knoester, Robinson, and Somé maintain that an important goal of schools in a democratic nation is to help students acquire the knowledge, attitudes, and skills needed to become informed, active, and efficacious citizens. They also envision schools as sites where students learn how to live and interact with peers from diverse racial, ethnic, cultural, and immigrant groups. The authors describe the challenges that schools experience in actualizing these goals, including the extensive racial and social-class segregation in U.S. schools that results in parents and families bringing divergent and conflicting interpretations and values to school–family discussions and interactions.

This book is designed to facilitate productive dialogues among parents, families, and educators, with a focus on immigrant students, students of color, and low-income students. In crafting this book, the authors drew on their personal and educational experiences as well as on theoretical and empirical research (Couchenour, 2012; Epstein & Associates, 2009; Galindo & Pucino, 2012; Knoester & Au, 2017). This book describes effective ways in which parents, families, and teachers can work together to enhance the academic achievement and the social and emotional development of students. The authors write, "Families, educators, and most of all, students benefit when families and schools work well together as partners toward the shared goal of supporting students" (p. 7).

The ways in which this practical book describes the challenges and possibilities that result when parents and teachers work together make it a timely and unique contribution to the Multicultural Education Series. The major purpose of the series is to provide preservice educators, practicing educators, graduate students, scholars, and policymakers with an interrelated and comprehensive set of books that summarizes and analyzes important research, theory, and practice related to the education of ethnic, racial, cultural, and linguistic groups in the United States and the education of mainstream students about diversity. The dimensions of multicultural education, developed by Banks (2004) and described in the *Handbook of Research on Multicultural Education, The Routledge Companion to Multicultural Education* (Banks, 2009), and in the *Encyclopedia of Diversity in Education* (Banks, 2012), provide the conceptual framework for the development of the publications in the series. The dimensions are *content integration, the knowledge construction process, prejudice reduction, equity pedagogy,* and an *empowering institutional culture and social structure.*

The books in the Multicultural Education Series provide research, theoretical, and practical knowledge about the behaviors and learning characteristics of students of color (Conchas & Vigil, 2012; Darling-Hammond & Darling-Hammond, 2022; Lee, 2007), language minority students (Gándara & Hopkins 2010; Valdés, 2001; Valdés et al., 2011), low-income students (Cookson, 2013; Gorski, 2018), and other minoritized population groups, such as students who speak different varieties of English (Charity Hudley & Mallinson, 2011), LGBTQ+ youth (Mayo, 2022), and students with disabilities (Waitoller & Thorius, 2022).

This book describes the ways in which structural and institutional racism casts a long shadow on school–family relationships. A number of books in the Multicultural Education Series focus on ways to lessen racism in educational institutions. These books include Ozlem Sensoy and Robin DiAngelo (2017), *Is Everyone Really Equal? An Introduction to Key Concepts in Social Justice Education* (2nd ed.); Gary Howard (2016), *We Can't Teach What We Don't Know: White Teachers, Multiracial Schools* (3rd ed.); Jabari Mahiri (2017), *Deconstructing Race: Multicultural Education Beyond the Color-Bind*; Zeus Leonardo (2013), *Race Frameworks: A Multidimensional Theory of Racism and Education*; Daniel Solórzano and Lindsay Pérez Huber (2020), *Racial Microaggressions: Using Critical Race Theory in Education to Recognize and Respond to Everyday Racism*; and Robin DiAngelo (2023), *Seeing Whiteness: The Essential Essays of Robin DiAngelo.*

Knoester, Robinson, and Somé maintain that it is essential for trust to develop between educators and families and across families in order to develop and sustain productive relationships that will facilitate the academic achievement and the social and emotional development of students. Teachers must also build trust with students. The authors also view the development of intercultural competences among students as an important goal of schools in a diverse democratic society. They write, "The development of intercultural competence, while not measured by standardized tests, includes knowledge, skills, and dispositions that will serve students throughout their lives" (p. 36). The authors advocate a critical multicultural curriculum that "will include aspects of the disgraceful history (and current presence) of White supremacy, along with anti-racist and culturally celebratory histories, art, and knowledge about people in our immediate and distant communities" (p. 38).

This practical book, which includes discussion questions at the end of each chapter, examines a wide range of topics about ways that effective relationships and communications between families and schools can be nurtured and improved. The authors describe and give concrete examples of how schools and families can work together to increase the academic achievement and the social and emotional development of students. I hope readers will actualize the authors' hope that this book will be read together in voluntary school-based book clubs or study groups that include families and educators. These book clubs and study groups should result in rich, engaging, and informative interactions and dialogues.

—James A. Banks

REFERENCES

Banks, J. A. (2004). Multicultural education: Historical development, dimensions, and practice. In J. A. Banks & C. A. M. Banks (Eds.), *Handbook of research on multicultural education* (2nd ed., pp. 3–29). Jossey-Bass.

Banks, J. A. (Ed.). (2009). *The Routledge international companion to multicultural education.* Routledge.

Banks, J. A. (2012). Multicultural education: Dimensions of. In J. A. Banks (Ed.), *Encyclopedia of diversity in education* (vol. 3, pp. 1538–1547). Sage.
Charity Hudley, A. H., & Mallinson, C. (2011). *Understanding language variation in U.S. schools.* Teachers College Press.
Conchas, G. Q., & Vigil, J. D. (2012). *Streetsmart schoolsmart: Urban poverty and the education of adolescent boys.* Teachers College Press.
Cookson, P. W. Jr. (2013). *Class rules: Exposing inequality in American high schools.* Teachers College Press.
Couchenour, D. (2012). Family diversity. In J. A. Banks (Ed.), *Encyclopedia of diversity in education* (vol. 2, pp. 882–884). Sage.
Darling-Hammond, K., & Darling-Hammond, L. (2022). *The civil rights road to deeper learning: Five essentials for equity.* Teachers College Press.
DiAngelo, R. (2023). *Seeing Whiteness: The essential essays of Robin DiAngelo.* Teachers College Press.
Epstein, J. L., & Associates. (2009). *School, family, and community partnerships: Your handbook for action* (3rd ed.). Corwin.
Galindo, C., & Pucino, A. L. (2012). Family diversity and school_family relationships. In J. A. Banks (Ed.), *Encyclopedia of diversity in education* (vol. 2, pp. 885–888). Sage.
Gándara, P., & Hopkins, M. (Eds.). (2010). *Forbidden language: English learners and restrictive language policies.* Teachers College Press.
Gorski, P. C. (2018). *Reaching and teaching students in poverty: Strategies for erasing the opportunity gap* (2nd ed.). Teachers College Press.
Howard, G. (2016). *We can't teach what we don't know: White teachers, multiracial schools* (3rd ed.). Teachers College Press.
Knoester, M., & Au, W. (2017). Standardized testing and school segregation: Like tinder for fire? *Race Ethnicity and Education, 20*(1), 1–14.
Lee, C. D. (2007). *Culture, literacy, and learning: Taking bloom in the midst of the whirlwind.* Teachers College Press.
Leonardo, Z. (2013). *Race frameworks: A multidimensional theory of racism and education.* Teachers College Press.
Mahiri, J. (2017). *Deconstructing race: Multicultural education beyond the color-bind.* Teachers College Press.
Mayo, C. (2022). *LGBTQ youth and education: Policies and practices* (2nd ed.). Teachers College Press.
Sensoy, O., & DiAngelo, R. (2017). *Is everyone really equal? An introduction to key concepts in social justice education* (2nd ed.). Teachers College Press.
Solórzano, D., & Huber, L. P. (2020). *Racial microaggressions: Using critical race theory to respond to everyday racism.* Teachers College Press.
Valdés, G. (2001). *Learning and not learning English: Latino Students in American schools.* Teachers College Press.

Valdés, G., Capitelli, S., & Alvarez, L. (2011). *Latino children learning English: Steps in the journey*. Teachers College Press.

Waitoller, F. R., & Thorius, K. A. K. (2022). *Sustaining disabled youth: Centering disability in asset pedagogies*. Teachers College Press.

Acknowledgments

All books are collaborative at some level. That is especially true for a book like this, written by three authors, working closely together. The information here comes not only from research literature but also from stories from our experiences as teachers, parents, and consultants to schools. We would like to thank all of the people we have worked with and learned so much from, and especially those whose stories appear in these chapters. Most of our family members are featured in a story here, but we would like to further thank all of our family members for their support throughout the writing of this book.

In addition, we would like to thank the people who have read and commented on earlier drafts, including Brian Bockelman, Ursula Dalinghaus, and Paul Jeffries. We would especially like to thank James A. Banks, who championed the idea for the book from the beginning and included it within his Multicultural Education Series, and to each of the editors we have worked with at Teachers College Press, including Brian Ellerbeck, Rupali Haldar, Alyssa Jordan, Jitendra Kumar, Gary Morris, Michael Olivo, and Nancy Power. Of course, any errors found in the book are entirely our own.

Introduction

> An individual has not started living until he can rise above the narrow confines of his individualistic concerns to the broader concerns of all humanity.
>
> —Dr. Martin Luther King Jr.

I (Maura) was 30 years old when I had my first child. I remember spending most of my pregnancy reading books about pregnancy, birth, and healthy eating, but it never occurred to me while pregnant to read about parenting skills, strategies, and expectations. When I arrived home from the hospital with my new baby, I looked at my husband and then at my beautiful daughter and asked, "What do I do now?" I felt clueless, unprepared, and lost about what I thought was my biggest responsibility in life. As they say, my daughter did not come with an instruction manual. My mother-in-law gave me the newest edition of Dr. Spock's book as a gift and told me to "use my instincts." I adored my mother-in-law, but I thought, "What instincts?" My own mother was in another country (Venezuela, where I lived until coming to the United States as a teenager to attend college) and unable to be with me. I did not know when (or if) my parenting knowledge was going to kick in.

I purchased all of the parenting magazines available at the time and read many books to arm myself for the task at hand. I asked my pediatrician a lot of questions. But in retrospect, I underutilized the most important resource of all: the wisdom, knowledge, and experience of other parents. Sure, I spoke to other mothers, friends, and family, but I never really asked them to share their parenting tips and secrets. It was a lonely time for me, because I could not "fess up" to my friends and family that I was flying by the seat of my pants. I did not want to look weak.

I had in my mind that having a child would give me magical wisdom and the skills needed for parenting, automatically providing the tools needed to help my daughter prepare for life and make sure that she eventually contributed to society, and most of all, that she would become a healthy and well-adjusted individual. At the time, I did not feel like I had any of those skills.

Despite my fears, I became my child's first and primary teacher. I learned by trial and error, and I believe many new parents are learning in the same way. I realize now that preparing my daughter for school started the day I brought her home from the hospital. I also learned to use guidebooks, websites, attend scholarly conferences, and spend hours reading academic research. But I also realize that many parents lose interest, time, and/or do not find these sorts of resources accessible.

When my daughter eventually grew to be school age, it became clear to me that there were not a lot of books or resources available addressing this transition, far fewer resources than were available for pregnant women or for new parents. Nor were there a lot of books available for parents of school-age children in general. In some ways, this makes sense. When parents send their children to school, they are entrusting them to trained professional educators. So as parents, we may feel our role diminishes. While this may be partially true, research has found repeatedly that the parenting of school-age children makes a significant difference in the academic, social, and emotional success of children and schools (Edwards, 2016; Epstein & Associates, 2009). But how can parents know how to support their children at this stage, and by extension, how to support the work of the school? That is where this book comes in.[1]

TRANSITIONING FROM NESTING INSTINCTS TO THE SOCIALIZATION OF SCHOOLING

The transition from home-based care to school-based care is part of a socialization process. It is natural that many parents

1. When we refer to "parents" here, and throughout the book, we mean any adult who is parenting a child, which could mean a large range of caretakers, not only biological parents.

experience "nesting instincts" as they start a new family. This first stage of parenting can be characterized as looking inward and providing comfortable conditions necessary for building strong attachments with the baby and among family members. By the time children reach school age and are ready for kindergarten—and for many families, this follows a period of day care or other care outside of the primary home—there is movement toward the child spending increasing amounts of time with greater numbers of peers and teachers.

There are few books written for this stage of parenting and for the stages that include middle childhood and beyond. This book was written to highlight, examine, discuss, and support this socialization process. During this time, there may be feelings of loss for parents and families, in the sense that they likely are not spending as much time with their child as compared to when the child was younger. There may be feelings of loss of control of the child's education. There may be questions, confusion, or disagreements with educators about many aspects of schooling. Yes, parents have spent many years attending schools themselves and know what attending school is like. However, few parents are professional educators or have been trained in education. We want to encourage parents to embrace and continue learning about this socialization period, because their involvement as parents is not any less important and because parents remain the child's primary and most influential teachers. The role of the parent and family remains extremely important, but at this stage it involves interesting new partners—trained teachers—with whom to collaborate.

Despite some misgivings, we also imagine that most parents look forward to this step in their child's development. It means their child will be in the caring hands of trained educational professionals. Parents will see significant growth in their child's abilities when they enter school, including academic knowledge and skills, such as learning how to read, count, add and subtract, name the days of the week and months of the year, and much more. Perhaps most importantly, and perhaps most enjoyable for children, they will make new age-peer friends and learn how to conduct themselves in ways that are conducive to large groups of people sharing a limited space. This is a big part of the socialization process at this age. As they continue their educational growth and development, they will be asked to speak so they are heard while not being interrupted, and to listen to others while not interrupting. They will learn to take care of individual and classroom materials, to provide a helpful hand toward tasks that benefit the entire class, and to speak publicly and perhaps even present to large groups such as the whole class or even the whole school.

COMMON QUESTIONS THAT ARISE FOR PARENTS

There are many questions parents may be wondering about schools and about education before their children enter kindergarten, and many more that arise once their child is in school. The questions and preferred communication approach may vary depending on various factors, including the families' ethnic background, education, country of origin, and socioeconomic status. Some of these questions may be relatively easy to answer, and a quick Google search, for example, a review of the school's website or handbook, or a call to the school or district office may provide enough information to satisfy parents' curiosities. Examples of such questions might be about enrollment procedures and deadlines, the school calendar, age requirements to enter kindergarten, transportation options, after-school options, required materials, breakfast and lunch options, how to contact a teacher, and options for additional academic or social support. Before enrolling, schools likely encourage parents to tour the school, and they may offer an open house where parents can meet the principal, the parent coordinator, and perhaps the kindergarten teachers to receive additional information.

Even before these questions arise, parents may be wondering about what type of school they would like to send their child. Depending on the location, a variety of options may be available. In many locations, a private or parochial school may serve a portion of students, likely charging tuition to the families that enroll. Approximately 10% of students nationwide attend private or parochial schools. There may be charter schools available, which are public schools that do not charge tuition to families. These schools (serving approximately 5% of students nationwide) receive their funding from the state (although there are exceptions to this rule) and are given autonomies that local public schools are not afforded, such as providing a unique curriculum and allowing families that live outside of the city in which the school is located to enroll their children. The autonomies afforded to charter schools depend on the state and locality, and not all states have passed laws allowing for charter schools. Another group of students, approximately 4%, are homeschooled by parents or by a group of families working together, and these students are not enrolled in a local brick-and-mortar school (although they may be enrolled in an online school) (Jamison et al., 2023; Schaeffer, 2024).

By far the largest group of students—approximately 82% nationwide—are served by regular public schools. These schools are generally funded by local property taxes, with additional funds coming from state and federal programs. Increasingly, public schools offer choice of schools within their districts, but they are mandated to serve all children who enroll in public schools. The authors of this book have experiences with and knowledge about each of these basic types of schools. However, since regular public schools serve the vast majority of students in grades pre-K–12 in the United States, we will focus most of our attention in this book on these types of schools. Even within these basic school types there are different emphases among schools and choices for families, regional differences, and variation in quality among schools.

We began this section with questions parents may ask that are straightforward and relatively easy to answer with a quick Google search or conversation with a teacher or administrator. However, the more one learns about education, schools, and their various approaches, the more questions likely arise. And these questions often become more complicated and harder to answer. In fact, some educators and parents may have such fundamentally different views that they may be irreconcilable. Examples of increasingly thorny questions might be: How can I best support my child's learning? What are the pros and cons of the various school models? Once I enroll my child in a particular school, can I also select my child's teacher? Can I freely enter the school building and my child's classroom at any time? Can I decide or influence the curriculum my child will be taught in school?

MANY PURPOSES FOR SCHOOLS

Before answering these questions, it is useful to take a step back to consider the purposes of schools. There are many reasons why communities collectively establish, support, and maintain high-quality schools. It might come as a surprise to some readers that public schools are a relatively recent invention, considering the long history of human civilization. It is only since 1918—just over a century—that all children in the United States have been required to attend elementary school. A strong movement pushed for child labor laws so children would not have to work in dangerous and low-wage jobs without opportunities to improve their life situations. Since then, the need for education has only increased. Post industrialization, the economy has become increasingly high-tech and more literacy and numeracy intensive. Most jobs today require a higher degree of literacy than they once did, and the jobs that pay family-sustaining middle-class salaries often require much higher levels of literacy, math, and/or scientific understanding and perhaps a college degree. Ordinary life has also become more literacy and numeracy intensive, and studies have shown correlations between education and increased health and longer life (Zajacova & Lawrence, 2018).

However, a high-tech, knowledge economy was not the original reason universal public education was created in the United States during the mid-19th century, when the common-school movement gained steam and the economy was largely agrarian. At that time, one of the primary reasons for pushing for widespread education, articulated by political leaders like Thomas Jefferson (although he did not live long enough to see universal public education) and Horace Mann, was because a democracy depends on an educated electorate. How were all voting citizens (as limited as suffrage was at the time) supposed to form political opinions and know how to vote if they were not able to read a newspaper? Of course, this was before the invention of television, radio, and the Internet. We argue that today, even with the many visual and audio informational sources available, democracy still requires education, perhaps now more than ever. Citizens in a democracy need to know how not only to read but to read "between the lines" of what politicians say, to fact-check what news sources and advertisers state, and to decipher whether sources and pieces of information are reliable (Knoester & Parkison, 2015). Further, an educated populace should be educated in the areas of history and sociology. The voting public can and should care about their own interests. But when we participate in politics, we are not only making decisions that affect our own pocketbooks, we should also be mindful of the other people with whom we live and whose lives our decisions may affect.

Previously, we described the socialization process that takes place when children first attend school. As children proceed, they learn how to share space with peers and teachers in a classroom and a school. This requires new and different behaviors and habits as compared to what is expected in the home. We want to encourage parents, educators, and others to think even more broadly about socialization. When children enter school, not only are they learning from peers and adults in the school, but the curriculum will also encourage them to learn about the wider world, its geography, its people, its history, and its art. As the great educator Paulo Freire wrote, students should be taught to read "the word and the world" (Freire & Macedo, 1987). Citizens in a democracy need to be socialized and learn how to play supportive roles not only in their families and among friends or classmates but also within their larger communities and even their state and country.

PARENTS AND TEACHERS

It is often said, including previously in this introduction, that parent involvement in schools is crucial to student success. One authority on family involvement in schools, Joyce Epstein (2009), wrote, "Partners [educators and families] recognize their shared interests in and responsibilities for children, and they work together to create better programs and opportunities for students" (p. 9).

We agree with this basic premise. Families, educators, and most of all, students benefit when families and schools work well together as partners toward the shared goal of supporting students. But the more one learns about the complex issues involved, the more one realizes that collaboration sounds easier than it is. Given their importance, these partnerships are worth deep reflection and intentional work to build. The difficulty of this task—despite its initial appearance as easy—is one of the main reasons we wrote this book, to help school communities make progress toward this goal through reflection and better communication.

Why might effective and trusting relationships between families and educators be difficult to achieve? There can be many reasons for distrust or, more bluntly, for cross-purposes. In her landmark book *The Essential Conversation: What Parents and Teachers Can Learn From Each Other*, Sara Lawrence-Lightfoot (2003) interviewed and observed both teachers and parents, with special focus on parent–teacher conferences. She analyzed and richly described how both educators and parents, with the best of intentions, can have a hard time understanding and trusting one another. Ominously, she wrote:

> Most parents and teachers will admit that despite the civil tones and the polite decorum characteristic of the exterior of most conferences, the space between them is full of mines ready to explode and that bloodshed is just as likely as balm, adversity just as likely as alliance. This portrayal of primal passion is rarely described in the literature on family-school relationships, where goodwill and good manners are assumed and prescribed. (p. 43)

As parents learn more about schools and their own children's experiences in them, questions about the schooling process increasingly emerge, often questions without easy answers. But it can be difficult to ask them or to have an open conversation with educators about sensitive issues without sounding disrespectful or perhaps judgmental of the teacher's or school's practices. There may be concerns, but parents may not know how to talk with their child's teacher without becoming emotional or confused about what to say or when or how to express their concerns. They may feel anger toward the teacher, for example, or guilty about their parenting, or perhaps wondering whether they are leaving their child in the right place for learning. Likewise, it can be challenging for teachers to raise issues that might sound critical of children without the parent feeling personally attacked or judged. Lawrence-Lightfoot raises a possible reason for distrust:

> When parents plead with the teacher to be fair to their child, they are usually asking for special consideration for their youngster.

> They want the teacher to consider the unique struggles and strengths of their child and offer a differentiated response. But when teachers talk about being "fair" to everyone, they mean giving equal amounts of attention, judging everyone by the same objective, universal standards, and using explicit and public criteria for making judgments. Fairness, for teachers, ensures a more rational, ordered, and dispassionate classroom. (p. 44)

It is possible to see here how these two parties could be working at cross-purposes, or perceive one another as doing so. Although they both may say they care above all for the "best interests of the child," they may be valuing different priorities and recommending different actions. This basic contradiction, which comes in many forms and specifics, is often hard to clearly explain and justify to one another. It can create blockages to more open and clear communication about other topics that might deepen the teacher's understanding of the child by learning from the parent, for example, or deepen the parent's understanding of the educational process by learning about the educational goals and strategies of the teacher and the requirements of the state or district. Due to a blockage of communication and inability or reluctance to discuss sensitive issues, distrust can grow.

Such distrust can also build when parents and teachers jump to incorrect and disrespectful assumptions about one another. Lawrence-Lightfoot notes that suspicion and wariness can increase:

> When there is an asymmetry between parents and teachers, it is difficult for the conversation to be productive and the relationship to grow. Bad things happen when teachers are made to feel like "the hired help" by powerful and influential parents. And raw feelings result when teachers flaunt their status, withhold information, and infantilize parents. (p. 49)

In these quotes, Lawrence-Lightfoot helps us to think about a few such possibilities for ways in which communication and trust can be elusive. The potential for cultural misunderstanding and stereotyping grows as well. Distrust often arises along power differentials and social patterns of marginalization, such as those based on race, gender, class, (dis)ability, nationality, language, religion, age, or other human differences, which can make communication even more challenging. Parents may be distrustful of schools because they did not have a positive experience in schools themselves as children. Teachers may be distrustful of parents because they perhaps never had to deal with some of the economic, social, educational, or cultural barriers that parents may be facing and teachers may make incorrect assumptions about them. But distrust is not inevitable, and it helps if educators and parents can thoughtfully reflect on both the importance of family and school communication, and if they work hard to imagine the perspectives of one another so open and respectful communication—and mutual learning—is more likely to occur.

ABOUT THIS BOOK

This book was written not only to be read but to be discussed. Ideally, we envision it to be read together in voluntary school-based book clubs or study groups that include both parents and educators. We cannot imagine a better way for sensitive and challenging topics about education and children to branch out to larger cultural and social issues. In fact, we have been involved with multiple book clubs with mixed groups of parents and educators participating, which were all positive experiences, although the chosen books were never written specifically for that purpose. The choice of the book matters—some may be richer or more relevant than others—but in these settings we have enjoyed some of the most meaningful and thoughtful discussions about potentially controversial and sensitive issues relating to education and parenting.

In a book club discussion, important and complex issues can be raised and discussed, and they do not have to be personal in the sense that the group is talking about a participating parent's child or about one teacher's practice or curriculum. There is space for people to raise ideas without taking the issues personally, unless a participant chooses to put themselves out there in that way. In a book club, especially one that includes both parents and teachers participating, and especially if the group is multicultural and mixed gender and diverse in other ways, participants can learn firsthand from the experiences and thought processes of one another. They can hear and use examples that are familiar to all involved based on shared experiences within a particular institution or shared local knowledge, which might help to facilitate communication and understanding. Reading and discussing this book ideally will deepen each participant's understanding of the complex educational processes, different parenting approaches, and the various cultural assumptions, understandings, and practices of others.

To help facilitate discussion, we have included discussion questions at the end of each chapter. We encourage readers to add to or change the questions as they see fit. The questions are tied to topics raised in the chapter and can serve as jumping-off points for further questions and discussion. If all goes well, we hope this book will be just the first that a voluntary book club reads together. We have added a list of books at the end of the last chapter that we recommend reading and discussing following this one.

ABOUT THE AUTHORS

The three of us have come together to provide what we hope will be a valuable resource for parents, schools, and ultimately for children. We each bring a broad set of experiences and knowledge to these issues. All three of us, along with our respective spouses, have raised children (Maura's daughter and Hervé's three children have all reached adulthood, while Matthew's two children are still school age). Each of us was trained in graduate schools in the areas of education and sociology, have taught in sociology and education departments in multiple colleges and universities, and have conducted research and have published in these areas. All three of us have either taught in K–12 schools or have worked extensively with schools and school systems as consultants and community members to improve family involvement, communication, and student success. And all three of us have longstanding interests in thinking about inclusion and responsiveness to diverse families in school spaces and about equity in education.

As mentioned previously, Maura immigrated to the United States from Venezuela as a teenager and raised a Latina daughter in schools in Indiana. Maura has built a business as a diversity, equity, inclusion, and belonging (DEIB) consultant and coach to school districts and organizations wanting to become more inclusive, particularly for diverse populations. She has also conducted research and written multiple books on these topics.

Hervé immigrated to the United States from Burkina Faso on being offered a Fulbright Scholarship to complete his PhD in sociology of education. Already a trained and experienced teacher in Burkina Faso and father of two children at that point (his third child was born in the United States), Hervé and his wife experienced becoming parents of school-age children in both diverse and majority White schools in New York, Wisconsin, and Burkina Faso. Hervé's experiences as a father, a teacher, a parent advocate, a scholar, and a college professor who specializes in diversity in education all bring insight to these issues.

Matthew was born in the United States to an immigrant father from the Netherlands (his mother was also born in the United States to a family that included a Dutch immigrant father). Matthew became a public school teacher, first at the secondary and then at the elementary level, primarily in the Boston Public Schools. He and his colleagues thought deeply about how to provide an equity-focused and inclusive school environment for children and families. His graduate work and research, including several previous books, closely examine multicultural schools, while his teaching of preservice teachers at the college level has also included significant attention to these issues. His two children are currently enrolled in the Milwaukee Public Schools.

This book is a reflection on our work as educators, parents, scholars, and activists for DEIB in education. The entire book was written collaboratively, although there will be stories or examples throughout the book that come from one of our experiences, and we will indicate whose experience that was. We hope the book will serve as a resource and communication tool for more thoughtful, intentional parenting of school-age children and for family–school partnerships that not only focus on the success of one's own child but also toward a more community-oriented viewpoint, mindful of all of the children and adults involved in education.

A SAFE PLACE FOR INQUIRY

Although the authors of this book are educational professionals and parents, and we make arguments in this book based on research and experiences, we want to be clear that we do not believe there is one right way either to educate students or to parent children. What we are discussing here is not religious dogma, and there is no heresy. Rather, we recognize that every decision in both education and parenting has trade-offs. We likely make decisions because at the time we feel the good elements outweigh the bad, but every decision likely limits further choices in the future, and we may find ourselves wishing we could change our minds later because it didn't turn out how we imagined. We often don't know the best decision beforehand, and we sometimes don't like any of the options available and feel trapped. Further, within families and schools, we are likely not alone in making decisions. We may need to go along with someone else's decision, whether that be a spouse, a partner, another family member, or in a school, the principal, colleagues, or educational policies or administrators higher up the line. It can be hard to take ownership of decisions if we do not feel a part of or perhaps even aware of the decision-making process. But this does not mean we as parents or educators don't make important decisions along the way; we certainly do.

In any case, we hope the discussions that happen around this book can be open and honest, that participants feel free to ask what they might initially think is a "stupid question" to reach deeper understandings, and that everyone involved will wade into the potentially troubled waters and learn something valuable from other participants, even if it is not what they thought it was going to be. Despite possible (or likely) disagreements or misunderstandings, we hope with deeper knowledge and reflection about the educational processes and people involved, reading and discussing this book will result in better communication, trust, and understanding, leading ultimately to more intentional decisions for children and their greater success in school.

DISCUSSION QUESTIONS

1. If you are a parent, what sources of information did you rely on in preparing to become a new parent?
2. If you used reading materials, such as books or websites, what do you remember about them?

3. Were you able to find any books or reading materials in preparation for sending your first child to school?
4. What other sources of information did you rely on for this later stage of parenting?
5. What questions did you have when your first child entered school?
6. How did you select a school for your child? What were your sources of information? What were you looking for?
7. What was the transition like for you and your family when your child went from being home or at day care to attending school full time?
8. Do you feel you are well informed about what is going on with your child at school?
9. What questions do you have about schools or education now?
10. What do you view as the central purposes of schooling for your family and for your child?
11. What do you view as the central purposes of schooling from the point of view of the larger city or community? In other words, why should communities collectively maintain and pay for public schools?
12. Do you see any gaps or contradictions between what a family may want from schools and what the community wants from schools?
13. If you are a teacher or member of the school staff, what further questions do you have for parents?

CHAPTER 1

Education for Democracy

> What, to the American slave, is your 4th of July? I answer: a day that reveals to him, more than all other days of the year, the gross injustice and cruelty to which he is the constant victim. To him, your celebration is a sham.
>
> —Frederick Douglass, 1852

In the introduction, we mentioned that one of the central purposes of schools in the United States is to educate for democracy. As we continue thinking about and discussing how schools are organized (we include more discussion questions at the end of this chapter), it is important to recall founding purposes. But democracy is not a straightforward concept. The idea is quite abstract, and the term "democracy" has different meanings to different people.

Abraham Lincoln at Gettysburg, for example, described democracy as government "of the people, by the people, and for the people." But as Frederick Douglass knew very well and pointed out in the opening epigraph, the United States has not always lived up to its ideals. While the United States has often been called a democracy, it is fair to say that democracy has never been fully realized. From the start, it did not include everyone. Only White men with property could vote (Keyssar, 2009). Slavery was legal and widespread. It took centuries of organizing, mass movements, a civil war, and continual struggle to inch toward a more inclusive representative republic. The nation has come a long way, but it has still failed to fully live up to the principles stated in the Declaration of Independence: "All men [and women] are created equal" endowed "with certain unalienable rights" and governments "derive their just powers from the consent of the governed."

Despite the country's failure to live up to these ideals, we argue they are still worth struggling for.

Fundamentally, democracy is a system of government dedicated to ensuring that power is never too concentrated in one person's hands or in too few people's hands (such as with a monarchy or dictatorship). The country's founders got that part right. Distributed power is important because power has the tendency to corrupt, and a single all-powerful ruler like a king or dictator (or concentrated power in too few people's hands) is generally too arrogant and self-serving to know and care about—and respond to the needs of—all of the people in the nation. This is assuming that the ruler is relatively benevolent. But history is also replete with all-powerful kings or dictators who were truly murderous tyrants.

More democratic forms of government were created with the understanding that checks and balances can provide more responsive government and civil rights that improve the quality of people's lives. Individual people and the communities in which they live know their own lives and their community's needs better than any distant politician can, so all citizens must have a voice and legal mechanism to make their wishes known and acted on. But civil rights for ordinary citizens need to be fought for and defended. Even with civil rights—such as the right to vote, the right to speak up against the government, and the right to practice one's own religion or to not practice religion at all—democracy depends on citizens being educated enough to know how to participate effectively to defend these rights, to learn about and to understand the issues being discussed, and to hold their representatives accountable to their own promises and to the preferences of the people. Although it may not have been apparent to the nation's founders, investments in education are not only necessary for democracy but benefit the population's health, life expectancy, and economy in many ways that were unforeseen (Dahl, 2015; Knoester & Parkison, 2017).

American democracy can still be improved to become more inclusive and responsive to the diverse constituencies it serves. It remains a work in progress. Most of these issues are beyond the scope of this book, but we would like to say more (and encourage discussion) about the educational needs of a democracy.

We want to be clear that we do not take democracy in the United States for granted. Two of us are immigrants from countries that have struggled—and have largely failed, especially in recent years—to secure democratic rights and freedoms for their people. We are Americans, all three of us, and care deeply about the democratic values in the United States, but we know the government and its traditions could be strengthened to become more inclusive and responsive to its people, to become "a more perfect union," in the words of the Constitution. We have also seen democratic norms, values, and laws slip away in countries that we love, and we do not want to see that happen in the United States.

EDUCATIONAL NEEDS OF A DEMOCRACY

In considering the educational needs of a democracy (as imperfect as it is), it is important to ask what kinds of knowledge and dispositions are necessary to become active and effective citizens. Unfortunately, evidence suggests that the educational preparation of current citizens leaves much to be desired (Knoester & Gichiru, 2021; Knoester & Kretz, 2017). Many studies have been conducted revealing alarming ignorance from ordinary people about basic governmental offices, functions, and history (Institute for Citizens & Scholars, 2018; Knoester & Parkison, 2017). Readers may even recall late-night television hosts using interviews with average citizens on the sidewalk to reveal ignorance of seemingly obvious facts for ridicule ("Who is the current vice president?" "Which party currently controls Congress?" "Against which country did the colonists fight the Revolutionary War?")

The lack of educational preparation of many U.S. citizens impacts democracy because without adequate education, citizens are unable to select representatives who vote and act in the people's interests. Citizens are easily conned by dishonest politicians and thus unable to hold their representatives accountable. But it is not just one's own personal interests that should matter to a voting citizen but the interests of their communities and of the entire nation and beyond. An enlightened and educated voting public should care about the welfare of more than themselves. We do not wish to pin all of the blame for lackluster democratic participation and citizen knowledge on schools, but schools can and do play a part. As James Banks (2007) reminds us:

> Citizenship education should also help all students, including mainstream students, to acquire the knowledge, values, and skills needed to interact positively with people from diverse ethnic, racial, and cultural groups and to develop a commitment to act to make their communities, the nation, and the world moral, civic, and equitable. (p. 2)

Citizenship education, we suggest, is the central reason that adults without children should and do pay taxes and vote to create policies that establish, maintain, and improve public schools, although there are also many other reasons for collectively investing in and improving schools.

In the introduction, we made the case for education looking outward rather than only inward, for offering more sociological and multicultural education to all students, along with the other core academic subjects, including mathematics, reading, writing, science, fine arts, and physical education. We want to be clear that we see no contradiction between schools pursuing both excellence and equity. Educators work hard both to meet the educational needs of all students and to offer top-quality educational opportunities, differentiated for students based on students' curiosities, knowledge base, and abilities. It is not easy to step into the shoes of another person. Educators need to think deeply about ways to enliven the curriculum so students can become more knowledgeable about the world and its people, history, geography, cultures, arts, technologies, and governments. Parents can support this mission by sharing their own knowledge and curiosities, sending their children to diverse schools, providing opportunities for cultural and academic learning outside of school, and encouraging their children to take these issues and academic subjects seriously.

DECIDING ON THE CURRICULUM

So, what does a school curriculum in a democracy look like? How is it decided? Parents may wonder why some subjects are given prominence while a particular subject they would like their child to learn is not taught in school. Why does the school teach x but not y? Subjects not taught in school might be highly beneficial for students to learn and may have powerful real-world applications. This is a frequent concern and topic of discussion within many school communities. Schools and districts must make difficult choices because, due to limited time and resources (especially teacher qualifications), schools cannot be all things to all people. It might be wonderful to offer a high-level bilingual program, for example, or instrumental music lessons, or computer programming, but hiring teachers qualified to teach in these areas may not be possible or realistic given resource constraints and competing priorities (Knoester & Meshulam, 2024).

For example, I (Matthew) come from a family in which several members, including my father and grandparents, immigrated from the Netherlands. As a child, I wanted to learn Dutch in order to communicate better with my grandparents (who continued to speak Dutch throughout their lives) and other relatives and to enjoy the benefits of learning more about my heritage and family culture. Unfortunately, no school I attended taught Dutch. If I wanted to learn Dutch, I would have to find opportunities outside of school, but those were not immediately available.

Similarly, as a parent, my children have found great joy in playing sports. They have enjoyed the physical education and extracurricular sports offered at their schools, and as a parent, I am grateful for these opportunities. In fact, in most countries, sports and academics are more separated than in the United States, where there are school-sponsored health classes and sports teams. Nevertheless, in the United States, despite the athletic offerings at schools, many parents, including myself, sign their children up for sports clubs, teams, or other recreation outside of school. Depending on the location, these opportunities can be relatively inexpensive, such as the recreation department of my city, which charges in the range of $25–$35 for a whole season's worth of instruction in sports. But the amount can also rise to many thousands of dollars per year for selective club teams with professional coaches, elaborate training facilities, and additional travel costs.

Each state has passed curricular standards in English language arts (ELA), mathematics, science, and social studies. These standards are easily found online by searching the state and the subject matter. The standards represent the academic priorities recommended for each grade level and toward which the high-stakes (such as student promotion and school evaluation) standardized tests are focused. We can notice, however, that there are no curricular standards that mandate high-level instruction in competitive sports, so it is reasonable that most schools, especially elementary schools, do not allocate their limited budgets toward these priorities. Although in some locations, particularly those with much higher budgets than that of my children's school, there are both public and private K–12 schools with state-of-the-art athletic facilities and highly competitive sports teams that train students nearly year-round. But this is an example of what most students do not have access to unless their families are able and willing to join a private and expensive league or club outside of the public school system.

So, a hard truth needs to be faced by all parents and educators: Schools cannot be entirely consistent with every family's culture and priorities. Scarcity of time and resources creates conflict because parents may assume that the school's role is to enhance their family's culture and priorities. Individual teachers and schools may attempt to do so, but they cannot be entirely consistent with everyone's family priorities. There needs to be some moderation, flexibility, and understanding on all sides (Kliebard, 2004).

This leads us to another hard truth about schools, which many educators find easier to avoid discussing: Education is a cultural intervention. This is true because what children learn in school would likely not be taught at home. Yes, parents might read with their children and teach them facts and skills, but the kinds of lessons teachers plan and carry out in schools are unlikely to happen at home. To the extent that the school's curriculum has an impact, it is culturally affecting the student, whether or not it is fully known and understood by parents and families. The deeper we examine this topic, the more we realize that it is almost inevitable that something a child is taught at school will not be agreeable to a parent (Knoester & Yu, 2015).

EDUCATIONAL GOVERNANCE

Returning to the topic of government, we recall that democratic governments were created to manage opposing viewpoints and to help facilitate people living together despite conflicts. It is sometimes forgotten that public schools are a part of a democratic government. In most locations, a local school board is empowered to make budgetary, policy, hiring, and curricular decisions based on votes from the community. The school board hires the superintendent, who is the chief executive of the school district.

Despite the democratic appearance of electing a school board, however, there are significant limitations to this process. Perhaps chief among the challenges to responsive government at this level is low voter turnout and the lack of knowledge of the voting public about the issues involved and the qualifications and stances of school board candidates (Meier & Knoester, 2017). Making school boards even less responsive to the voting public, there has also been a move toward consolidation of school boards, such that in some locations the school board is appointed by a mayor and in other locations there is only one school board for an entire state or other large area (Henig & Rich, 2003). Nevertheless, the governmental structure of public schools, however imperfectly, serves to create school policies that are responsive to the needs of the voting public.

A scholar who has thought deeply about how schools can operate fairly while attending to each of the constituencies involved with schools is Amy Gutmann. In her book *Democratic Education* (1999), Gutmann offers a well-thought-out theory and rationale to understand and justify the various roles involved. She proposes a democratic model, which contrasts with competing positions that foreground either families, the state, or individuals as the sole or primary decision-makers about school issues (which she refers to as the Family State, the State of Families, and the State of Individuals). Gutmann's democratic model consists of shared decision-making among the key stakeholders in education, bound by two basic principles. Those are *non-repression*, which implies that students and teachers should have the right to discuss and learn about competing notions of "the good life" in schools, and *nondiscrimination*, which means all students must be given the opportunity for an effective education. These principles hold that particular stakeholders (such as parents or government officials) should not overstep their bounds, that a central purpose of public education is teaching children about various views of the "good life," that all children have the right to be educated, and that all stakeholders in public education must cede at least some control of educational decision-making to professional educators (Gutmann, 1999, pp. 41–47). This is an important point, since parents of students outnumber professional educators (including staff and administrators) by large margins, so a democratic education does not necessarily mean that every member of the school community has the same amount of influence within the school.

Just as governments were created to slow down the process, to avoid concentrated power, and to create more deliberate policy, so too do schools and school systems have checks and balances among their multiple constituencies. This might seem unfair (why should other people decide what happens with my children in school?). But power is distributed among the stakeholders, and there are multiple shareholders and people with differing levels of input/decision-making power within the system.

Due to the checks and balances implemented, no one constituency can, acting alone, implement a highly controversial policy. And, ideally, due to the deliberation required, parents and others may be more likely to understand the policy. In practice, school systems and entire states have adopted curricular standards, which set priorities for school learning, but with vague enough wording that there are many ways educators can create lessons addressing the standards. Schools and teachers are expected to tie their lesson plans and units to particular curricular standards in each of the core subject areas. These standards provide a sort of political cover for teachers. While teachers attempt to create engaging and differentiated lessons for their students, drawing on culturally relevant pedagogy and knowledge about the particular interests and curiosities of students, they must also be able to say that they are teaching lessons tied to the curricular standards that have been adopted by the state or district.

Tensions nevertheless arise, tensions within the school or school system, parental disagreements with the curriculum, disagreements with a teacher, disagreements with a principal, or perhaps tensions among parents. All of this is to be expected and is not necessarily negative, especially if mutual understanding can eventually be reached. There is a delicate balance to be struck, and we might critically ask, "Whose culture is given greater worth than others? Whose curriculum is being taught?" (Apple, 2014). The curriculum has been an area of continual struggle over time (Kliebard, 2004). Meanwhile, students are also developing their own agency away from their parents and families, perhaps creating greater cultural conflict from the viewpoint of a parent.

Due to these kinds of disagreements and tensions within public schools, we can see that many parents (approximately 18%) choose to send their children to private or parochial schools, charter schools, or homeschool their children. Still, all parents who send their children to public schools, parents who do not send their children to public schools, and even community members without children in schools have the right to make their voices heard regarding public school policies.

BOOK BANS AND OTHER VIOLATIONS OF THE PRINCIPLE OF NON-REPRESSION

For example, as we write these words, there are heated debates taking place and recently passed laws in multiple states banning specific books in schools and libraries. Although over 70% of parents oppose book banning, according to a recent survey conducted by the American Library Association (2022), many hundreds of books have been banned from public and school libraries in recent years (Hlywak, 2022). PEN America (2023), a free speech organization, created an Index of School Book Bans that lists "1,477 instances of individual books banned, affecting 874 unique titles" within that year. They state: "Overwhelmingly, book banners continue to target stories by and about people of color and LGBTQ+ individuals."

While these book bans may have popular support in particular locations, it is clear to us that they violate Gutmann's principle of non-repression. As a reminder, this democratic principle holds that students and teachers should have the right to discuss and learn about competing notions of "the good life" in schools. Competing notions of the good life discussed in schools might challenge each child's home culture. But the work of schools is not merely to replicate each child's family's values, which, given the diversity represented in schools, is a logical impossibility. It is to empower students to think for themselves, to make new relationships with people different from themselves and to learn from them. We encourage parents—of all races, ethnicities, sexual orientations, and socioeconomic backgrounds—to embrace these learning opportunities for our children and hope that the new ideas our children encounter are intriguing, challenging, stimulating, and that they help our children to grow in their critical thinking abilities and desire to continue learning about the world and the people in it.

Gutmann laid out a theory for an equitable distribution of decision-making about school issues when the purpose of education is for democracy. However, when considering school policies, one must have more than ideals. What is also needed is a clear-eyed critique of what currently exists and about the obstacles that may endanger the pursuit of education for democracy. Research suggests social inequalities found outside of school have enormous impact within schools and among schools. These inequalities continually threaten Gutmann's principles of nonrepression and nondiscrimination.

UNEQUAL SCHOOL BUDGETS

Despite the gains that have been made in terms of the provision of universal public education throughout the United States, inequalities abound. Different schools and school systems have vastly different budgets, for example, depending on local property taxes and other funding mechanisms. While some schools are allocated less than $10,000 per pupil, other schools are allocated more than $60,000 per student. Differences in funding strongly correlate with school outcomes. A study conducted by Rich et al. (2016) found that "sixth graders in the richest school districts are four grade levels ahead of children in the poorest districts." This study also found racial disparities: "There are large gaps between [W]hite children and their Black and Hispanic classmates. The gaps are largest in places with large economic disparities." Jonathan Kozol (1992) put a sharp point on his analysis of school disparities when he wrote:

> What is now encompassed by the one word ("school") are two very different kinds of institutions that, in function, finance and intention, serve entirely different roles. Both are needed for our nation's governance. But children in one set of schools are educated to be governors; children in the other set of schools are trained for being governed. The former are given the imaginative range to mobilize ideas for economic growth; the latter are provided with the discipline to do the narrow tasks the first group will prescribe. (p. 176)

Funding disparities and the narrowing of the curriculum for poor schools, as described by Kozol, are disturbing on multiple levels, including violating Gutmann's principle of nondiscrimination. Every student should be educated to be an effective and productive member of a democratic society—a "governor"—with opportunities to become economically successful, healthy, and live long lives. The "savage inequalities," in Kozol's words, of school disparities create enormous disadvantages for students whose families are already struggling to survive and to make ends meet. These are large structural issues to which we will return in Chapter 6, suggesting ways parents and educators can be active in supporting their local schools.

CONCLUSION

In this chapter, we discussed how and why schools attempt to manage the different viewpoints and priorities of various constituencies. Public schools are imperfect institutions with limited budgets (some more limited than others) and cannot be all things to all people. But they are inclusive in the sense that they do not turn families away and are the schools perhaps most likely to be culturally diverse and integrated, with opportunities for students to build intercultural competence. The curriculum does not always reflect all families' values and priorities, and parents may feel the need to supplement what their children are learning in school with outside academic or recreational activities, or at-home discussions, readings, and experiences.

In the next two chapters, we discuss in more depth the power of integration and intercultural competence to improve school communities and their outcomes. This will be followed by a chapter focusing on how schools and parents can communicate more effectively about the curricular offerings at the school so parents can better support their children's learning. We then turn to how schools and parents can find themselves working at cross-purposes and how they might reach common priorities and goals. We move on to ways parents can be involved and active in improving their schools and the larger community's educational offerings. We further suggest ways that parents and educators can advocate for policies at the city level that might assist both schools and families while being mindful about equity and inclusion.

DISCUSSION QUESTIONS

1. What did you think about the topics in this chapter? Have you witnessed any of the phenomena described here?
2. What do you think are the educational needs of a democracy? What is the minimal amount of education required for a democracy to function? Would more and better education improve democracy? If so, in what ways?
3. In your view, who seems to make most of the decisions about schools and education? What do you know about the local school board and superintendent?
4. Take the time to search for the state standards in each subject by grade level in your state. What do you notice about how the standards are written, and what seems to be included or excluded?
5. You may have heard the saying "the apple doesn't fall far from the tree," referring to how children tend to become like their parents. How do you think this metaphor might relate to teaching and learning and the parenting role?

Can you think of ways in which the metaphor rings either true or false in your own life or with the people you know?

6. What do you think might be a common misunderstanding among parents and teachers about schools or about one another?
7. What additional questions did this chapter raise for you?

CHAPTER 2

Integration and Intercultural Competence

> In schools we have an opportunity to teach the coming generations to preserve and extend the United States as an experiment in building a democratic community. The task is far from over, and the victory for democratic pluralism is far from certain.
>
> —Duane E. Campell (2010, p. 13)

As parents choose a school for their children, several factors come into consideration. One of the factors parents often consider in selecting a school (along with a neighborhood in which to live) is racial and socioeconomic diversity. The demographic makeup of schools is generally available online, along with test scores and reputational analyses.

The demographics of the nation and of schools are dynamic and vary considerably among locations. For the first time in U.S. history, White students, or students of European descent, are no longer in the majority nationwide. Further, nearly 1 in 4 students in U.S. schools are members of families with at least one immigrant parent (Camarota et al., 2023). Schools in nearly all locations are becoming more diverse, although, as Frankenberg and Orfield (2007; 2012), remind us, they remain racially and economically segregated.

DEMOGRAPHICS AND SEGREGATION

Seventy years after the Supreme Court decision *Brown v. Board of Education,* in which the court ruled that "separate educational facilities are inherently unequal," the United States continues to struggle with segregated schools (Orfield et al., 2019). Politically, this issue has been placed on the back burner, with rare mentions of this decision in the current press, but we do not want to lose sight of it. This chapter focuses on (and encourages discussion about) why the integration of schools continues to matter and continues to be a goal worth striving for. Follow-up questions arise: Why has racial segregation in schools persisted 70 years after *Brown v. Board of Education*, which was meant to desegregate schools? Why is racial integration in schools on terms of equality so challenging but still worth fighting for? We explore these questions and more throughout this chapter.

According to surveys of parents, a strong majority say they are in favor of integrated schools (Lake Research Partners, 2023). There also seems to be a stigma against White parents openly saying they prefer racial segregation (Knoester & Au, 2017). Still, judging by actual patterns of where families live and where they send their children to school, segregation persists. Segregation in housing is also a vestige of racist policies like redlining and restrictive racial covenants that are now illegal, but they set in place patterns of segregated housing (Rothstein, 2017).

As Orfield et al. (2019) report, "One way to measure segregation is through the concentration of non-[W]hite students in schools. . . . Since the peak of desegregation for [B]lack students in 1988, the share of intensely segregated minority schools, that is, schools that enroll 90–100% non-[W]hite students, has more than tripled from 5.7% in 1988 to 18.2% in 2016." The data are not so simple, however. Schools with majority White students are less likely to be entirely White than they once were: "During the same period, the share of intensely segregated White schools, that is, schools that enroll 90–100% White students, has declined from 38.9% in 1988 to 16% in 2016" (Orfield et al., 2019, p. 21). These findings reveal that in many locations, perhaps especially rural and small-town areas throughout the United States, schools are less likely to be entirely White given the growing diversity in many parts of the nation and growing diversity in the nation as a whole, even as metropolitan schools remain highly segregated.

Segregation poses serious challenges to the goal of education for democracy. Considering the growing cultural diversity of the United States, students need to make connections with people different from themselves in order to develop intercultural competence and to overcome negative stereotypes. As Hawley et al. (2007) suggest, diverse and integrated schools are worth struggling for: "The development of intercultural competencies, such as the capacity to work well with persons of different races, appears to require practice, and thus cannot be learned in homogeneous schools" (p. 33). Not only does this make intuitive sense, but there is robust research supporting such claims.

BENEFITS OF INTEGRATED SCHOOLING

Scholar Rucker C. Johnson (2019) conducted an extensive study to better understand the effects of integration in schools. He found striking results in favor of integration. For example, his study found that desegregation fundamentally affected the educational resources students received, which corroborated the Supreme Court's claim that "separate educational facilities are inherently unequal":

> Almost as soon as desegregation plans were enacted, there were not only substantial reductions in racial segregation, among both students and teachers, but also sharp increases in per-pupil spending (by an average of 22.5 percent) and significant reductions in the average class sizes experienced by [B]lack children. (p. 58)

Because this research was longitudinal, Johnson was able to study not only academic gains for all students but long-term effects for students educated in both segregated and desegregated schools. He found a set of striking measurements related to long-term economic benefits to graduates of integrated schools. It is fair to question whether these findings are correlations but not causations, but they are noteworthy nonetheless:

> We discovered that the average effects of a five-year exposure to court-ordered school desegregation led to about a 15 percent increase in wages and an increase in annual worktime by roughly 165 hours, which combined to result in a 30 percent increase in annual earnings. Furthermore, the average effects of a five-year exposure to court-ordered school desegregation led to a decline of

> 11 percentage points in the annual incidence of poverty in adulthood and about a 25 percent increase in annual family income. . . . For African-Americans, exposure to desegregation beginning in the elementary school years, instead of attending segregated schools alone, led to a reduction of 3 percentage points in the annual incidence of incarceration and a decline of 22 percentage points in the probability of adult incarceration. (p. 62)

There were also long-term emotional and mental health correlations:

> Exposure to integrated, well-funded schools predicted lower adult rates of hypertension, cardiovascular disease, and obesity (which is among the leading causes of death in the United States). The precise causal mechanisms behind these specific outcomes cannot be fully understood from our analysis alone. . . . Importantly, we once again see the consistent absence of any significant impacts on [W]hites across these adult outcomes—whether in terms of educational attainment, earnings, poverty, or incarceration rates. This finding flies in the face of the fears that many [W]hites held about integration as they predicted it would have negative effects for [W]hite children. (pp. 64–65)

These findings are consequential. Emotional and mental health benefits are critically important. In a separate study, a large majority of parents reported highly valuing their children's learning of social and emotional skills at school. "About two-thirds of parents of K-12 students (66%) say it's extremely or very important to them that their children's school teaches them to develop social and emotional skills" (Horowitz, 2022).

Given the research on the positive effects of racial integration in schools, it should not be surprising that other institutions, including for-profit companies, have also been found to perform better with a multiracial staff (Cunningham, 2009; Richard et al., 2007). As Carucci (2024) summarizes, "the data are unmistakably clear. Companies committed to diversity and inclusion significantly outperform those that aren't." In fact, this is the main reason that both for-profit companies and non-profit organizations have hired Maura and her company to offer training in DEIB as professional development for their employees for 3 decades.

My company (Maura), Inclusion and Beyond, Inc., provides coaching and consulting services to for-profit and not-for-profit organizations around the country. Part of my work is to help management and employees understand cultural competency as a behavior-in-action instead of thinking of it as a feeling. I have found that once they understand the root of cultural competency, that is when the work begins. Management and employees need cultural competency tools to show them how individual behaviors impact and create a sense of belonging within the workplace.

For example, one tool that can be used in teacher education or professional development to test one's unconscious cultural biases is the Intercultural Development Inventory (IDI). As an assessment tool, the IDI measures an individual's or groups' progression along a developmental path of increasing complexity called the Intercultural Development Continuum (IDC). This standardized assessment can be administered as a pretest and posttest before and after diversity training to help teachers and others critically reflect on their own biases to better meet the needs of their students and families. Another useful assessment tool was developed by Project Implicit, which provides a free online survey testing one's implicit cultural biases: https://implicit.harvard.edu/impl.

These assessments and related research findings have demonstrated that the benefits of racial integration and development of intercultural competency are not limited to childhood or to academic gains. The knowledge, skills, and dispositions necessary to work within multicultural settings are worth developing from a young age and have lifelong positive outcomes. We should not be complacent with the current state of segregation in schools but should encourage parents to choose multicultural schools for their own children and support such schools in their communities. For those of us who have children in integrated schools, let us not take this aspect for granted or let it languish. Let us work to make these schools, and all schools, more respectful, inclusive, and welcoming places for all students and families.

Despite the positive gains found in research on integrated schools, it is important to not overlook the troubling way that *Brown v. Board of Education* was carried out. We know, for example, that after the 1954 Supreme Court decision, segregated Black schools were almost entirely closed down and more than

38,000 Black teachers, and hundreds of Black administrators, lost their jobs (Horsford, 2011). These schools were assets to their communities, and their closing and the loss of these jobs were devastating. Further, the Black students who integrated previously all-White schools often faced hostility, discrimination, and separation even within "desegregated" schools (Oakes, 2005; Walker, 2000). In many cases, these patterns have continued. We do not wish to sugarcoat this painful history.

Further, we do not argue that an integrated or desegregated school necessarily leads to positive sociocultural understanding. As Hawley (2007) explains, "Bringing students of different racial and ethnic backgrounds together in schools creates opportunities that then must be used wisely to achieve positive outcomes" (p. 32). All students must be treated with respect, dignity, and caring attention. Everyone's cultural background deserves respect and is a source of knowledge to build on as a strength, not a weakness. As Edwards (2016) suggests, effective teachers learn about these cultural funds of knowledge, inquire and follow up on various aspects of the diversity present among students in order to best teach them:

> The school demographics can provide much information regarding income and statistics based on the cultural makeup, but teachers need to dive deeper into that information. For example, are the language learners in your classroom from an area outside of the United States? If so, are they immigrants or refugees? Are they proficient readers in their first language? Having that knowledge will assist you in connecting with parents and, ultimately, in determining how you will address the students in your classroom. (p. 12)

These questions do not answer themselves. An integrated school provides opportunities and challenges for teachers and students to learn from one another in multiple ways, but productive educational environments require intentional development.

Regarding the demographics of the teaching force, Zippia (2024) reports there are approximately 4 million teachers employed in the United States. Roughly 74% of teachers are women, while approximately 26% are men. According to Schaeffer (2021), the most common race or ethnicity of public school teachers is White (79%), followed by Hispanic/Latino (9.0%), Black or African American (7%), Asian or Pacific Islander American (2%), Native American (1%), and two or more races (2%). Due to these demographics, despite continuing segregation, it is likely that students of color will have White teachers and that White teachers will teach students of color.

We realize this is a simplified way of looking at ethnic and cultural differences. The truth is that many races, ethnicities, cultures, languages, religions, sexual orientations, abilities, and other human differences are represented in schools. Diversity can present challenges both to communication and to building trust, but also powerful opportunities for all involved (including parents) to learn from one another and to grow in intercultural competence (Frankenberg & Orfield, 2007; Howard, 2020).

Whether schools are more or less diverse, a curriculum that includes the study of various cultures, histories, sociology, and against negative stereotypes and implicit biases increases the likelihood that children learn powerful intercultural competencies. There are many ways to do that within a thoughtful curriculum. As James A. Banks (2019) explains:

> [The] research indicates that the use of multicultural textbooks, simulations, multicultural media, and cooperative teaching strategies that enable students from different racial and ethnic groups to interact positively can help students develop more positive racial attitudes. These kinds of materials and teaching strategies can also result in students choosing more friends from outside racial, ethnic, and cultural groups. Curriculum interventions such as plays, folk dances, music, and role-playing can also have positive effects on the racial attitudes of students of elementary schools. A major goal of the transformative multicultural curriculum is to help students understand how knowledge is constructed, how school knowledge usually reflects the perspectives of the mainstream and dominant groups within society, and how the experiences of minority groups are often marginalized within textbooks, within the school curriculum, and within society writ large. (p. 41)

Unfortunately, the belief that diverse and integrated schools with multicultural curricula are inferior or less desirable is widespread, although we argue such a view is misguided (Knoester & Au, 2017). Segregation persists, even in integrated neighborhoods. It is important to continue to question why that is. One possibility is that some parents (and educators) believe that excellence and equity are at odds with one another. In other words, there is an assumption that working toward integration and intercultural competence within schools somehow compromises academic quality. This belief may be a natural result of the way that academic performance is measured. Integration and intercultural competence are not valued as key focuses of school policy, nor considered in the rankings of high schools, such as that found in *U.S. News and World Report*, for example. Federal, state, and district policies place heavy weight on standardized test scores, which do not value or attempt to measure integration or intercultural competence. Narrowly focused standardized tests incentivize schools to ignore the importance of integration and intercultural competence (Knoester & Au, 2017; Meier & Knoester, 2017).

The choice between equity and excellence is a false dichotomy; they are not mutually exclusive. Racially integrated schools in which students of all races and backgrounds are treated with equity provide many benefits. Whether it is out of morality and a sense of equity and duty to the larger society, or out of self-interest, it is advisable that even people from dominant cultural groups develop more intercultural competence. Today's students, regardless of background, are likely to work in multicultural settings, even if they are currently living in segregated neighborhoods. They will know a country that is even more diverse than the one we, as adults, inhabit. Despite the fearmongering around this issue, we know that parents can still help guide their children to college from an urban public school, for example, and students can achieve other outstanding successes. The development of intercultural competence, while not measured by standardized tests, includes knowledge, skills, and dispositions that will serve students throughout their lives, including in increasingly diverse higher education settings, a diverse job market and workplaces, and more diverse communities and states. Whether one is supportive of these processes or resistant, these are social realities, and our communities and our children benefit if we take sociological knowledge and intercultural competency seriously.

INTERRUPTING RACISM

Earlier in the chapter, we discussed the social stigma of parents stating openly that they choose segregated schools for their children. Choosing racial segregation for segregation's sake is not a polite thing to say. Studies have found there are coded ways to speak about deeply held racist beliefs. For example, since standardized tests are strongly correlated with race and class, parents and others can refer to test scores as their determination of the quality of a school, and about their choice of school for their children, without even mentioning the racial and class demographics (Bonilla-Silva, 2013; Knoester & Au, 2017).

Despite the stigma in many circles, we also know there is openly spoken and displayed racism present in many of our communities. Although legalized racial segregation and the killing of Black and Brown people with impunity are much rarer than they once were under Jim Crow, openly racist statements, beliefs, and actions persist (Kendi, 2016). We can close our eyes and pretend that these beliefs and actions do not exist, but we know better. For example, all of us have likely seen people fly Confederate flags from their trucks or homes, and we know from news reports (if not from personal experience) that Nazi symbols continue to be displayed and found—including in and around schools (Laguarda, 2024). In broad daylight, we have likely seen revolting bumper stickers on cars driving by, and other openly racist statements made online and in the media. Mass shootings continue to take place, including within Black churches and in heavily populated stores with Black and Brown people, and within synagogues (Southern Poverty Law Center, 2024). News reports indicate that parents of shooters are nearly always "shocked" that their child could do such a thing. So let us not be so "polite" as to pretend that these hateful sentiments and actions are not still with us. These examples once again underline for us the importance of critical multicultural education.

In fact, we are going to go out on a limb and assume readers of this book do not want our children to be demonstrating White supremacist beliefs and behavior at all. This behavior is not sanctioned by schools in any of the locations with which we are familiar. But we must ask, what are the educational implications of ensuring our own children will not harbor these kinds of beliefs—which they almost certainly will encounter—and that they understand that White supremacist beliefs are morally wrong and harmful not only to the larger culture but to themselves? The answer is not to remain silent about these phenomena and to pretend that they do not exist. Multicultural education is essential.

Some parents may believe that anti-racism "goes without saying," maybe because it is "obvious." However, we also know that many children not only see the aforementioned racist symbols but are likely coming across videos or reading hateful and racist (and sexist, and otherwise discriminatory) messages online without their parents' knowledge. Therefore, adults need to be proactive in sending anti-racist and anti-discriminatory messages to children. A critical multicultural curriculum will include aspects of the disgraceful history (and current presence) of White supremacy, along with anti-racist and culturally celebratory histories, art, and knowledge about people in our immediate and distant communities. The good news is that multicultural education is not drudgery. It includes countless joyful aspects of cultural and human differences. It may be useful to remember that there is a reason many people choose to travel and to experience different cultures, for example. Immersing oneself as a minority in another culture is often enjoyable, festive, and jubilant, while also creating lasting and impactful relationships and memories. This is one example of an action that parents can take in exposing their children to and learning together about cultures different from one's own. Other actions parents might take to improve their children's intercultural competency include reading books aloud together that are written by multicultural authors and/or with multicultural characters, participating in extracurricular sports or activities that include people from various cultural backgrounds, socializing with a larger range of people than what a child might encounter at school, listening to music from a variety of cultural traditions, visiting museums or cultural sites with children that celebrate various cultures and knowledge, and having conversations at home with children that show respect and interest in learning from people different from one's own culture.

CONCLUSION

This chapter has focused on the importance of understanding school integration and the development of intercultural competence both at school and at home. Of course, these issues affect all families differently. For example, given disparate cultural assumptions and modes of communication, diverse families may encounter different challenges, such as not knowing how to communicate with White teachers to create partnerships. Speaking personally, as a diverse parent having a child in a mostly White school, I (Maura) was petrified at first when I needed to communicate with my daughter's teacher. I am sure that I was not the only one to feel this way.

Even as an educated mother who had lived in the United States for many years, I was apprehensive about approaching a teacher if I had a concern. One of my concerns was how approachable the teacher was going to be and wondering whether I would offend her with my questions. And if so, would she take it out on my child? Some families come from cultures in which questioning teachers is disrespectful, and sometimes students suffer repercussions because of this. Transitioning to American educational structures and norms is not easy for many parents, and it may take time for families to learn to trust the teachers and the school system.

In the next chapter, we delve further into these ideas and discuss some of the personal experiences that Hervé and his family have had in U.S. schools, coming from Burkina Faso and living as Black Americans in multiple locations in the United States.

DISCUSSION QUESTIONS

1. What do you view as the central purposes of schooling from the point of view of teachers?
2. Have you ever taken a class on sociology? Do you agree that greater understanding of demographics, culture, and patterns in society may be beneficial not only for individuals but for the larger society? If so, in what ways?
3. What keeps you up at night when you think about your child's education?

4. In what ways might equity and excellence be at odds with one another, and in what ways might they not be?
5. In what ways have you seen the segregation and/or desegregation of schools play out in your lifetime?
6. What are examples of multicultural education—learning about someone else's culture—that were meaningful and memorable to you? How can you imagine children experiencing something similar?

CHAPTER 3

Education and Culture

> People are competent, they have knowledge, and their life experiences have given them that knowledge.
>
> —Norma González et al. (2005, pp. ix–x)

In the previous chapters, we discussed the main purposes for schools and raised cultural and racial segregation and inequality as key challenges to effective schools for multicultural democracy. In this chapter, we extend our argument (and encourage discussion) about how schooling is a socialization process, worthy of reflection and investment from all involved. Socialization is not only about children making new friends at school, although that is important. Schools are also places where children (and adults) learn to respect, appreciate, and come to understand the knowledge and struggles of people who are culturally different and have different experiences from themselves. Knowledge and appreciation about different cultures, or intercultural competence, can and should become increasingly sophisticated as children grow older, but it is not inevitable. Noticing cultural differences can just as easily lead to disrespect as to appreciation and a source of valuable knowledge. Intercultural competence requires intentional work and should be part of a school's curriculum, which educates for democratic citizenship.

COMING TO THE UNITED STATES

I (Hervé) come from a place, Burkina Faso, a country in West Africa, that is quite different from the United States in many respects. When I describe the cultural situation in which I grew up, I have discovered it is hard for many people in the United States to comprehend. My parents never went to school, and they did not speak French, which was the language used in the nation's schools. While most of my early schooling was in French, I also studied and learned English and eventually became an English teacher. My parents did not speak English either. The fact that they neither spoke nor read in French or in English was a challenge when it came to supervising their children's homework.

Nevertheless, they imparted to me the idea that I should take my schooling seriously. They constantly reminded me that if I failed at school, I would have to come home to take part in the family's onerous farming activities. To me, farming in Africa back then looked very much like forced labor, as farmers tilled the fields with rudimentary tools under a scorching sun. My parents were also not content with fearmongering. They would see to it that I studied my lessons at home every evening. They would even flip through my notebooks to make sure I was serious about my work. While they were totally illiterate, they would rebuke me if they felt I was being sloppy with my writing. Their intuitive sense of aesthetics would signal to them whether I was putting in all of my effort. Back then, students were not using ballpoint pens but pens dipped in inkpots, and teachers would not tolerate any ink blots on the lessons that were copied from the blackboard, nor would my parents.

I tell this story about my own socialization for multiple reasons. I have found that many educational professionals, and indeed, mainstream discourse in the United States, tend to assume that because some parents—such as my own—are not literate or have not gone very far in school, that their knowledge is not useful to their own children's education. The assumption seems to be that parents must have a college degree or be professionally trained educators to positively influence their children's education. However, this is a deficit view of parents (Valencia, 1997). It does not recognize the knowledge that all parents have, regardless of their economic or educational background. Although my parents could not read or write, they nevertheless valued education and took many actions that positively contributed to my education.

I still vividly remember our family gathering around a fire, under an inspiring moonlit compound, listening passionately to the story of Daa palèrè (the equivalent of the proverbial Ananzè, the king-trickster always ridiculing Hyena). Little did I know that these formative years in oral literacy were preparing me to develop my command of French at an early age. Skills are transferable, indeed. I quickly excelled in "redaction." Students found this specific primary school assignment daunting, as it required them to create an essay out of thin air. No rubric was provided. A typical prompt might be: "You went hunting with your dad in the forest. Tell us the story." Since I had been fed on family storytelling, it was easier for me to tap into my imagination to come up with a coherent and cogent story that had a moving power. On many occasions, I was made to read my redactions in front of the entire class, which was not insignificant for my little ego. My oral literacy at home was a bridge to my formal literacy at school. This is a reminder for schools to espouse a capacity—rather than deficit—model as they interact with and seek to learn from students and parents, since knowledge can be developed in many different ways.

Still, my educational journey was a long and challenging one. It involved running to school—several miles there and back—literally barefoot when I was a young child. It required avoiding poisonous snakes that lived along the journey to school. It included countless hours of arduous studying of a language—English—that was not spoken in my village. Still, with the support of my parents and others in my community (we all know the Kenyan proverb "it takes a village to raise a child"), I was able to become a teacher and eventually a Fulbright Scholar and professor of education in the United States.

I am trying to be humble here. I am not saying that I am some kind of superhero. But it is important for me to recognize where I come from. Educational research or perhaps common sense might suggest that my story is impossible. It is true that parents tend to make a significant difference in the educational trajectories and lives of their children, but we should not assume that parents who are not formally educated themselves cannot significantly support the formal (and informal) education of their children.

Educators and parents can assume that students like myself are not likely to be found in most schools across the United States. That assumption is true if taken literally—there are not a lot of immigrant children from rural Burkina Faso in the United States. However, schools here are becoming increasingly diverse, and the stories of some of the children and their families may be equally hard for many Americans to comprehend. There is not one cookie-cutter definition of what an American student or family looks like or what they have experienced.

UNDERESTIMATION OF PARENTAL KNOWLEDGE

Perhaps due to my unlikely story of having come to the United States from rural Burkina Faso, I have spent a large portion of my life, especially in the United States, being underestimated. I have noticed other people of color, immigrants, and those from lower socioeconomic backgrounds being underestimated and undervalued. I have come in contact with many people in the United States who assume that my knowledge of Africa, including knowledge that is valued in Africa, is not real or valuable knowledge. No matter where one comes from, including Africa, all people have knowledge. But the knowledge and strengths of all students and families are too often incomprehensible, inaccessible, or not seen as valuable to teachers and to the school establishment. Inequalities we see in school outcomes may not be because families and students lack knowledge but because their knowledge is not recognized and valued by the "official curriculum" (Apple, 2014; Compton-Lilly, 2002).

All of this is not to say that school knowledge is not important; it certainly is. Curricular standards have been crafted based on deliberation among school officials and professional organizations. These standards compile knowledge and skills understood to be most beneficial to students in higher education, in various careers, and as citizens. The challenge is for teachers, students, and parents to work together to leverage the knowledge students bring from home and their life experiences, connecting what they already know with the content standards that educators are expected to teach and students to learn. This is one of the reasons why communication and trust between schools and families is critically important. Parents, educators, and students have much to learn from one another as they attempt to maximize student learning (González et al., 2005).

Both teachers and parents are interested in and concerned about how students learn the curricular standards in school. But this process can be incomprehensible to parents and students. In fact, even college-educated parents may not be in a position to fully assist their children at home to the extent educators—or other parents sending their children to the same school—may expect. Some parents may simply be too daunted or overwhelmed, confused about how to do so, or assumed it is the teacher's job to take care of the entire task of formally educating their children. Still, this does not mean their children cannot succeed in school.

As children advance in grades, parents helping them at home can become even more of an uphill task with the growing difficulty of subjects. But parents should not throw up their hands. They can still help by encouraging students to put the necessary effort into their work and by clearly communicating the idea that it takes 99% perspiration and 1% inspiration to succeed, as Einstein taught us and as my own parents reminded me. In the chapters that follow, we will provide many more ideas and tools for how parents and schools can work both together and separately to support student learning.

There is no denying that both parents and teachers contribute important elements to the education of children. As scholar of parent–school relationships Patricia A. Edwards (2016) noted, "There is a need for doors to be reopened in both directions, and, as my mother said, parents need to help the teachers to help their children. Teachers and administrators need to help parents know how to do that" (p. xviii).

WHEN PARENTS MAY NEED TO SPEAK UP ON BEHALF OF THEIR CHILDREN

As newcomer immigrants to the United States, my wife and I were fortunate to both hold graduate degrees. As professional educators, we became savvy to the educational system, especially in terms of the uneven and inequitable outcomes for students based on class, race, ethnicity, and other characteristics. When the time came, we felt the need, and were mostly able, to help the teachers of our children readjust their decisions that we felt were not always in the best interests of the children, although we do not believe the teachers were acting out of malice. It is our belief that because we did not allow all of our children's teachers' decisions to go unchecked, we were also providing lessons for our children as well. Yet we wonder about the thousands of families that have not been able to wield the same influence or were not willing to come to the school to check on their children.

As alluded to in the previous section, many parents do not become directly involved with their children's school, not because they do not value education as we might be tempted to conclude, but perhaps due to logistical or time constraints, or because they have had negative experiences with schools themselves, which have taught them to stay away. Further, in many cultures, the teacher is understood to be all-knowing, and parents have no say in the formal education of their children. Some parents may further feel insecure with their command of the English language or the right vocabulary. Due to lack of adequate funding, schools cannot always avail themselves of translators for parents who do not speak English. In many such cases, the student is relied on to serve as the translator, which can be humiliating for the parents, whose authority may be understood to be subverted.

Allow me to share a personal story that illustrates misunderstanding between the school and family. One of my sons is a quiet boy. He would rather spend hours reading than talking to adults. As previously mentioned, he is from a multilingual family but has only a working knowledge of French, the language most often spoken by his parents, although everyone in our family is also fluent and comfortable in English. When he was in 2nd grade, my wife and I went to school for a parent–teacher conference. The teacher was nice with us and showcased his work. She was positive about our child in general, but at the end of the conference she encouraged us to meet with her again in a month because she felt that our son was lacking social skills. Although this rubbed us the wrong way, I maintained my serenity and asked what exactly she found to be a red flag. She said that his wrist seemed not strong enough for writing and that he could also be suffering from what she called social muteness. She believed that the fact he came from a bilingual family could be connected to his muteness.

After a month, my wife and I went again to meet with our son's teacher. When we arrived, we found two other adults in the room with her. The meeting started without the two new people even being introduced to us. The teacher went straight to the point and informed us that our child was going to be placed in an ESL (English as a second language) classroom because he comes from a bilingual family. He was also going to be placed in Title I, as he was on a reduced lunch. Moreover, he was going to be referred to a special education classroom. And without further ado, we were handed documents to sign to mark our agreement.

I must confess, I was flabbergasted. I asked the teacher of record to tell me who the two other figures were. One was the principal and the other was a school counselor. I politely but firmly declined to sign, pointing to the clearly flawed process. I told them that minoritized students (racially and socioeconomically) were overrepresented in special education classrooms, in part, due to rash decisions like this.

Teachers may have at heart the best interests of their students, but if they are not careful, cultural dissonance and misunderstandings can lead them to misconstrue differences in communication styles between several cultures as problems in need of remedy. We know all too well the danger of trying to fix what is not broken.

My wife and I denied the intervention, and our son nevertheless did very well in school. In fact, he was identified as a gifted student in math and English. Yet we encountered additional problems with the school. Approximately 1 year after the aforementioned incident, we learned that our son would be removed from the gifted math program but without the teacher directly informing us of this. When we finally discovered this move, we wanted to know more. Our son told us that one day, as the gifted math teacher came into the classroom to lead the students to a separate room, our son was told to remain in his seat when he stood to follow the rest of the gifted students. He confided that this made him feel embarrassed and confused.

I sent an email to the teacher and the principal to let them know I was not happy about the way my son was removed from the gifted program. It was only then that the teacher let me know that my son was struggling with some concepts and that she thought it was in his best interest if he was removed from the program, to become better prepared before coming back. I replied that I did not believe this and that I would really appreciate it if my son was returned to the program, lest I make a fuss about the situation. To the school's credit, our son was reinstated into the gifted program, and he thrived until he graduated. Eventually he was accepted and entered into a prestigious university, focusing on math and computer science. Years have passed since this series of events, but I still have these emails with me, as they remind me of the struggles we faced as parents.

We not only intervened in our children's schooling to stick up for them when we felt they needed more decent treatment. On several occasions, my wife and I volunteered in our children's schools. I remember speaking several times in my children's classrooms about what life was like in Africa, the good and the bad alike, as Americans tend to know only about the terrible stories coming out of Africa. I presented in classes about French colonialism in Africa and the lingering effects these practices have had on contemporary Africa. I also remember serving as a "mystery reader" in one of my children's classrooms, reading a children's book about life in Tanzania. My son seemed proud to be put on a pedestal that day.

These examples are in no way meant to diminish the virtue of teachers or of schools. All of my children's teachers have taught my children—and our family—a great deal. I am profoundly grateful for their work. The stories I share are merely meant to highlight the complexity of this exercise and the possibilities for misunderstanding, despite good intentions. It is common sense that students learn from teachers and that parents can learn how to best support their children from their children's teachers and from the school's communications. However, what is too often neglected, and the point we are making here, is the fact that teachers and schools can also learn from parents and families, and this knowledge can be used to more effectively teach children.

WHAT CAN TEACHERS AND SCHOOLS LEARN FROM PARENTS AND FAMILIES?

Parents, even as they may be willing to work with teachers, may not have the same concerns, expectations, or communication styles. Cultural differences can have a significant effect on communication and how educators, parents, and students understand one another (Somé & Orelus, 2015). Of course, there can be many definitions of culture. Hofstede et al. (2010) suggest that "although the variety in people's minds is enormous, there is a structure in this variety that can serve as a basis for mutual understanding" (p. 4), so it is worth deeply considering how cultural differences may play out in schools. Hofstede et al. further note:

> Culture consists of the unwritten rules of the social game. It is the collective programming of the mind that distinguishes the members of one group or category of people from others. Culture is learned, not innate. It derives from one's social environment rather than from one's genes. Culture should be distinguished from human nature on one side and from an individual's personality on the other, although exactly where the borders lie between nature and culture, and between culture and personality, is a matter of discussion among social scientists. (p. 6)

Further, some cultures are considered "high context" and others more "low context." In a high-context culture, the situation will dictate expectations more than words. A "yes" is not necessarily a "yes" and a "no" is not necessarily a "no." An answer of "no" may be understood to be causing another person to lose face, such as in particular Chinese understandings of Confucianist philosophy, which emphasizes harmony, with the focus being on the group rather than the individual (Hofstede, et al., 2010). How is a teacher to know this, one who is likely socialized in a low-context culture, such as in the U.S., wherein communication is conveyed mostly in words.

Allow me to share another personal example that illustrates this point. I remember fondly my graduate study years, when I first arrived in the United States, and we international students were frequently invited to share meals with our instructors. There was food galore, but many of us (those from more high-context cultures) would nevertheless return from the party with disappointment and even hunger. In many cultures, when invited to eat in someone's home, the guest is expected to express some kind of restraint by not serving themselves as much as they may wish to eat. It is expected that the host insists, so the guests can then eat their fill. American instructors, in contrast, would ask us international students to serve ourselves once. When we said we were okay, they would not insist, leaving the impression that we were not genuinely welcome to eat as much as we wanted. On the other hand, the American instructors would feel disappointed that so little food would be eaten, which they interpreted, incorrectly, to mean that we were not happy with what was being served. Differing cultural dimensions can lead to a breakdown in communication.

Turning again to schools, parents and students are not always invited or forthcoming in sharing their knowledge and cultural understandings, so educators may not perceive cultural misunderstandings that have taken place regarding their children. In order to foster greater understanding of cultural assumptions for the purpose of building relationships and for creating curricular units that might foster greater engagement for students and broader shared knowledge, educators may need to conduct outside research. Teacher education programs in undergraduate and graduate programs, including the programs in which the three of us authors have taught, include courses on multicultural education and intercultural competency. However, the cultural knowledge and understanding that might be beneficial in schools is infinite and is worthy of ongoing research and learning throughout one's life. Aside from ordinary conversations and interactions, ongoing research focusing on cultural groups represented in the school might also include reading professional books or articles, watching films, attending workshops, traveling to a variety of locations with disparate cultures, and otherwise seeking information from knowledgeable people. It helps if a school can collaboratively gather and share this information and continually work together to deepen everyone's knowledge, understanding, and appreciation for the cultures represented in the school rather than leaving this work to one individual teacher. We will return to this topic in the next chapter.

CULTURALLY RESPONSIVE TEACHING

Culture shapes our beliefs, values, and social practices, and structures ways of life that are not easily changed. Students in our classrooms bring this culture with them as a base of knowledge, much of it unconscious (González et al., 2005). When discussing this issue, many White students in the United States, including some in our college classes, bemoan the idea that they do not have a culture, assuming instead that only racial and ethnic minority groups have culture. Nothing could be further from the truth. Culture starts within the family and is also shaped by our home neighborhoods, our larger communities, and society (Gee, 2015). Ethnicity, gender, religious affiliation, (dis)abilities, sexual orientation, socioeconomic status, age, regional or national origin, language, and other factors are all markers of culture.

As Banks (2003) notes, "The nation's deepening ethnic texture, interracial tension and conflict, and the increasing percentage of students who speak a first language other than English makes multicultural education imperative in the 21st century" (p. vii). This is true because while many people experience cultural diversity firsthand, understanding and cultural appreciation do not necessarily follow such interactions. According to Ladson-Billings (1995), multicultural education, or what she calls "culturally relevant pedagogy," should be a crucial aspect of effective teaching. Culturally relevant teaching validates students and their cultural understandings on terms of equality and encourages teachers to offer opportunities for students to build on and extend their bases of knowledge. The fact that our schools are made up of many cultures is not in dispute, which makes more responsive pedagogies a necessity. Cultural knowledge is legitimate knowledge. This does not mean that one culture is better than another. But culture is a resource from which students can draw and potentially find inspiration. Further, understanding culture and cultural differences is important not only for teaching but also for many kinds of encounters between various cultures, useful for life beyond school.

THE VALUE OF ACADEMIC LANGUAGE IN SCHOOLS

One key aspect of culture is language. While it was declared the official language of the United States by executive order only recently (March 1, 2025), English has been predominantly used for centuries, including in business, in government, and as the language of instruction in most schools. Students (and their parents) who come to school in the United States unequipped with standard English have been at a disadvantage. They are perforce lacking in this precious cultural capital that puts their more fortunate peers far ahead. Let us use the analogy of currency here. Knowledge of another language, excluding academic English, is like having millions of cedis (the national currency of Ghana) in America. This will not help in the United States. One may have money, but it is useless in this location.

Students (and their parents) who come to school with a less valued linguistic capital than academic English are not limited to newcomer immigrants. The pool of such students and families is wide. Among others, there are African Americans, Native Americans, and many students coming from working-class families. They may speak English, but there is a dissonance between their vernacular English and the standard English taught in the school systems. It is fair to say that many American-born students can be understood to be linguistic immigrants within the school setting. But schools must meet the needs of all linguistically diverse students and to learn to work effectively with their parents as well.

It is therefore crucial that all involved with schools understand how this diversity can present challenges in communication and building trust, yet this diversity also presents a valuable opportunity for all involved to grow in intercultural competence. The development of bilingualism, for example, can have powerful social and economic benefits (García, 2009). Still, just because diversity exists in a school does not mean that bilingualism or intercultural competence will develop. To use a metaphor, just because one has eggs, flour, sugar, and baking powder does not mean they have a cake. It must be intentional work.

We want to be clear that we do not mean that the United States is a "melting pot," to use the old metaphor. There is nothing wrong with cultural differences; the idea is not to erase differences. Cultural preferences, traditions, and beliefs are sources of strength for individuals and communities. However, building intercultural competence means taking the time to learn about cultures that are different from one's own, to appreciate and understand the value they hold for individuals and communities, and to work to create bridges of communication and understanding. In an educational setting, it means teaching children in ways that allow them to learn from their own families and traditions, find overlaps that connect personal interests or cultural knowledge with the academic subjects being taught in school, and attend to the positive identity development of children.

Please allow me (Maura) to share a relevant story here from my experience. As a diversity, equity, and inclusion consultant for a rural school in Daviess County, Indiana, I was assigned to work with a teacher in charge of students who did not speak English as a primary language. My job was to provide her with the tools and the strategies needed to be more successful in communicating with students and parents. She did not speak any of the six different languages and eight dialects spoken by her students and parents in her school at that time. She and I worked on the differences in family practices, languages, customs, and traditions of her students and parents. I asked her to research the villages and cities of origin of her students and parents to help her understand them better. Following considerable research, she eventually became recognized as an expert in communicating with her students by learning unspoken rules of their cultures, while spoken language became a secondary concern. For example, she learned the different cultures' hand, head, and facial expressions and movements. She came to understand whether the family structures were more matriarchal or patriarchal. She learned about the customary foods and the differing meanings of the word "no" used to show respect or politeness. She also helped families to become more knowledgeable about the laws, schools, and culture of rural and urban areas in the United States by facilitating their attendance at various workshops and sessions. Intercultural competency can include the commitment to learning a foreign language, but there is much else, as illustrated in this example, to learning forms of communication and understanding used by various cultures.

CULTURE AND ECONOMIC INEQUALITY

As implied with the metaphor of the foreign currency, culture is not neutral but carries power, and not all cultures have the same currency everywhere. This is in part because people from particular cultures are disproportionately affected by economic hardship and poverty, including Black, Latino, and Native

American groups in the United States. But we must be mindful that cultural groups are not devalued and disrespected within our schools due to the various hardships experienced by people from these cultures. Bourdieu and Passeron (1977) argued that the success of students in schools is strongly correlated with the value the school places on their cultural capital. It follows that students whose cultural capital is less valued will experience what Bourdieu and Passeron call "symbolic violence," blaming the children and their families for their failure to embody the dominant (White) cultures. Educators must be aware of and counteract these dynamics. As Berger and Riojas-Cortez (2016) suggest:

> In order for teachers to engage parents in the education process, they must develop sociocultural consciousness. In other words, they need to understand the inequities in society (Villegas & Lucas, 2007). Teachers need to develop such understanding because they need to learn how to reach parents and how to get rid of negative stereotypes. Before teachers develop this type of understanding, they must know their own identity and biases, then they can understand and even appreciate the children they teach and their families. (p. 7)

As part of professional growth, teachers can and should reflect on where they came from, the habits and routines in their family, their community and the values that were dear to them, bringing what is unconscious to consciousness. Knowing oneself starts with an intentional exploration of oneself. It is not a matter of common sense, just as it is difficult to stand on a balcony and see oneself walking in the street. All these elements have an enduring influence on who we are as humans, our likes and dislikes, judgments, and recommended courses of action. We may not understand why we behave the way we do, as habitus or our identities make us believe that our behavior is natural and inevitable when, in fact, they are a set of socially constructed dispositions that structure our behavior and preferences (Bourdieu, 1977). A teacher's unexamined culture made of likes and dislikes, norms and values, may become a hindrance to student learning.

Sociocultural knowledge entails awareness of sociological patterns, not only about culture but includes understanding the prevalence of economic hardship and poverty ubiquitous in society and in schools. Approximately 16% of all children in the United States are living in poverty (Kids Count Data Center, 2021). As Matthew Desmond (2023) describes:

> This is who we are: the richest country on earth, with more poverty than any other advanced democracy. If America's poor founded a country, that country would have a bigger population than Australia or Venezuela. Almost one in nine Americans—including one in eight children—live in poverty. There are more than 38 million people living in the United States who cannot afford basic necessities, and more than 108 million getting by . . . in that space between poverty and security. (p. 6)

Educators, parents, and other adults involved in schools should avoid assigning blame to families for real or perceived hardships. Since their salaries generally align with a middle-class standard of living, it is possible that teachers have never experienced economic hardship and are unaware of the ways that parents and families strategize and must make difficult choices and sacrifices to survive. Gorski (2018) correctly identifies negative judgments of parents living with economic hardships as a deficit perspective:

> Deficit ideology is a blame-the-victim mentality . . . the natural inclination of the educator who ascribes to deficit ideology is to believe that parents experiencing poverty show up less often because they do not care, because they do not value education. . . . Across the U.S., schools invest time and resources in initiatives designed to solve a problem that does not exist, not only wasting time and resources, but also risking further alienation of the most marginalized families. (pp. 60–61)

Gorski has described teachers with awareness of these misunderstandings or critical social consciousness as "equity literate": "Equity literacy is the accumulation of these kinds of bigger contextual understandings essential to our growth as equitable educators and leaders (Gorski & Swalwell, 2015; Swalwell, 2011). I define it as *the knowledge and skills educators need to become a threat to the existence of bias and inequity in our spheres of influence*" (p. 17, emphasis in the original).

Gorski's research focuses on the work of educators to develop sociocultural awareness. However, this work can also be part of the long-term learning of students, as their sophistication grows, and part of the messaging to parents from the school. We also hope that parents view fellow parents generously and value the diversity of experiences that are represented in an integrated school (Johnson & Nazaryan,2019).

Given the challenge of surviving and thriving in the current economy, it should not be surprising that studies suggest some parents, particularly economically struggling families, are less likely to attend school functions and to communicate with the school. But this does not mean that these parents do not care about their children's education. As Gorski (2018) explains:

> Imagine, if you haven't experienced it, that you are an economically marginalized parent of two elementary school children. You *want* to attend events at your children's school, but you work the evening shift at your second job. And because you're a wage employee, you don't have paid leave, so missing work means losing wages, which, by extension, could result in another late electricity payment: bad news with winter approaching.
>
> Remember, now, that your poverty—or, more specifically, the economic injustice that propels poverty—means that you are more likely than wealthier people to work multiple jobs, including evening jobs. . . . Regrettably, this is one of many obstacles you face in attempting to engage with your children's school. You might not be able to afford child care or transportation (Jarrett & Coba-Rodriguez, 2015). Have the people scheduling these events ever had to rely on public transportation? You wonder, trying to calculate the least expensive and most time-efficient bus route from your first job to the school, then to your second job. (p. 115)

Not only are economically struggling parents less likely to attend school events, but noted sociologists Annette Lareau and Wesley Shumar (1996), who conducted in-depth studies on this question, concluded, in part: "working-class and lower-class parents often fear school authorities, perceiving the school as a potential threat in their lives" (p. 33). There are multiple reasons for these fears, perhaps chief among them being that the school could call Child Protective Services and have children removed from the home if school personnel believe they are not treated appropriately. Although the possibility may be faint, parents know that their parenting is being judged and that it is possible—even likely—that they are misunderstood, misjudged, and undervalued as parents. Increasing expectations of family involvement is therefore not an easy solution, as this can heighten the fear. All of these factors, and others, create uneven opportunities for parents and families to participate in the life of the school and for educators to learn from families.

The social consciousness just described entails the belief that learning should not be understood purely in cognitive or academic terms. But learning is also relational (Noddings, 2013). Unfortunately, schools have frequently placed too much emphasis on thinking processes. Students and families bring their "whole selves" and should be recognized and nurtured as such. Building trust is a key component.

CONCLUSION

Although this chapter has largely addressed the needs of teachers to develop intercultural competence and to be continually aware of cultural differences and inequalities, we also ask that parents appreciate and reflect on these dynamics as well. We hope parents will recognize this work as essential to what schools do.

Another central message we wish to send here is one of encouragement, especially for parents who may be struggling. We know—from personal relationships and from research—that there are parents who are feeling inadequate or even guilty about their parenting or about their finances or their overall well-being. They may feel it is nearly impossible to make ends meet or that due to lack of time or resources they are not able to offer their children the opportunities they would like. They may wish their children had two active parents rather than one, for example, that being a single parent is somehow inadequate. Perhaps they wish they had more support from extended family or from the "village," better transportation options, healthier food, a bigger home, better health care, more opportunities to take vacations and/or to travel, more resources for summer camps or sports or arts camps, or in other ways not doing enough for their kids. There is always something more that parents could be doing for their children. The people reading this book may not feel this way. But we know there are large numbers of parents who do.

We would like to say to all parents (all people parenting children)—that you are enough. You are what your children need. And beyond that, you have a deep wealth of knowledge that your children need and can benefit from. Further, the school and the larger community can benefit from your knowledge, experience, and wisdom. It may not be easy to come to school events, to participate as a guest speaker or as a chaperone on class trips, to fill out surveys or to attend parent–teacher conferences. But please do not discount your knowledge, although you may receive messages to the contrary. For the remainder of this book, we will discuss these issues further and suggest ways that sharing information and knowledge between parents and educators and among parents might be done in more efficient and effective ways for busy people.

DISCUSSION QUESTIONS

1. For parents: What do you wish the school or your child's teacher knew about your family or your child?
2. In what ways do you think parents might be misunderstood by other families or by the educators at the school?
3. For educators: What do you wish the parents of your students knew about you or about the school?
4. In what ways might educators be misunderstood by parents and families of the school?
5. Explain the metaphor about having eggs, butter, flour, sugar, and baking powder doesn't mean you have a cake. How might this metaphor be related to an integrated and multicultural school?
6. What are examples you have experienced that may have helped you to develop intercultural competency?

CHAPTER 4

Improving Communication Between Families and Schools

> Parents tell us that feeling welcome and being treated with respect by school staff is the number one key to their connection with a school. When school staff construct caring and trustful relationships with parents, treating parents as partners in their children's education, parents are far more likely to become involved—and stay involved.
>
> —Anne T. Henderson, et al. (2007, p. 47)

In this chapter, we focus on (and encourage discussion about) how schools and parents can communicate more effectively so they can learn from one another and work together toward the shared goal of educating the children in their care. We discuss some of the traditional ways educators and parents communicate, such as with school newsletters, parent–teacher conferences, school events, student performances, robocalls, and websites. We also suggest that schools can improve these forms of communication and add additional methods to optimize communication and collaboration.

What do all parents and educators need to know about high-quality communication? Building trust between schools and families is multilayered. On the one hand, it has to do with articulating and coalescing around a vision for the school and building mutual understanding. It also involves listening to one another and valuing the knowledge and experiences that are brought by each party. In order to enact a powerful educational vision and work toward shared priorities within a school, ongoing communication is key, but different forms of communication also have various benefits and limitations. As Murphy and Torre (2014) summarize:

> To create a culture of engagement, leaders implement policies and practices that accommodate varied family structures and needs. This includes extending available times for conferences to allow working parents to participate, hiring interpreters to aid with communication with non-English-speaking parents, implementing culturally responsive family nights, and/or providing transportation to school events (Powell, 1991). Activities for parent involvement can be academic or nonacademic. Their purpose is to nurture collaboration between parents and students, parents and teachers, and students and teachers. (p. 183)

In this quote, the authors suggest a variety of ways that schools and families can communicate. Including both academic and nonacademic content emphasizes that communication and collaboration are not restricted to schoolwork but focus on building a relationship of trust, which can open lines of communication. In the sections below, we outline some of the major forms of communication that schools practice, with suggestions about how to make the most use of them.

ONE-WAY COMMUNICATION: NEWSLETTERS

One common method of communication schools use is an online or paper newsletter or bulletin. These newsletters often share essential information and can be written by classroom teachers, the school staff (such as principal or other administrators), district administrators, parent volunteers, or a combination of people and offices.

Newsletters are a useful tool for articulating the school's vision and its methods for achieving it. It is helpful for the leadership of the school to flesh out how vision or mission statements are enacted. School newsletters provide opportunities for school staff to describe and illustrate the school's curriculum and focus, to let parents know about upcoming events that parents and families are invited to attend or access, to introduce families to the staff members themselves, and much else. There are logistical issues that are important to communicate, and there are resources available to families that the school might inform parents about via the newsletter or bulletin.

We also know there are limitations and potential drawbacks to relying too heavily on newsletters. Newsletters are a one-way form of communication, so they can unintentionally send the message to parents that they do not know much and only the school holds information and knowledge. In our experience, newsletters tend to be too focused on logistics and not enough on curriculum. Perhaps their greatest drawback, however, is that they often never reach parents (if they are paper, as opposed to electronic, they likely rely on a child to take them home, which might never happen), and parents can be too busy to sit down and read them. Likewise, if the newsletter is sent in an email, those emails may never be opened. If the newsletter is posted on a bulletin board at school, parents may not enter the school building, notice it, or stop to read it. Schools cannot depend entirely on newsletters to communicate important information.

Beyond concerns about whether newsletters reach parents or parents have the time or energy to read them, they remain important opportunities to communicate with parents who are available and interested in the information included. Of course, thoughtfulness is required to build trust and a reliable readership via newsletters. Our overall concern about newsletters or bulletins is that they are too often treated like an afterthought. Yes, they often communicate the essentials: logistics, such as registration procedures, required permission forms, transportation issues, before- and after-school options, needed materials, when and where events are taking place, and so on. These are important aspects to include in them. But an opportunity for deeper collaboration that could be taking place centered on curriculum is often missed, even as we know not every family reads the newsletter.

If schools are explicit about curriculum and they communicate well how and why they are teaching the way they are, parents can be solicited to work as partners in educating their children, supporting and encouraging them at home in a way the school is unable to do but in ways that greatly support their child's learning. For example, if schools can encourage families to read at home with their children and provide resources to do so, studies have shown that this can positively and substantially affect a child's learning in school (Logan et al., 2019). If a parent knows a child is studying a particular topic at school—for example, ancient Egypt—the parent might ask the child questions about it, share their own enthusiasm for the topic, suggest that they watch a film about it, read a book about it, or even visit a museum together with objects related to ancient Egypt. Teachers and parents working together toward a similar goal for children can have the effect of supercharging the student's education.

Unfortunately, schools often miss this opportunity. Given the pressures of running a school, it is not easy. Rarely is a full-time, professional-level educator with excellent writing skills, time, and deep knowledge of the curriculum—including the specific lessons that are taking place in the classrooms—employed as a communicator with parents. The principal or office manager is often the main communicator, although many teachers send periodic newsletters, but people in each of these positions are often overwhelmed and distracted by their many other responsibilities. Administrators and office managers often lack detailed knowledge about the curriculum. Communication with parents about the education of their children, and the ability and time necessary to effectively build collaborative relationships and genuine understanding with parents, go missing.

I (Matthew) had the unique opportunity of working as a teacher for 5 years in an elementary school led by Deborah Meier as the principal. Meier was named a MacArthur Fellow (often called the "Genius Award") for her leadership in schools, serving as principal first in three schools in New York City and later a fourth school in Boston, which defied the odds in terms of rates of graduation and other positive outcomes (Knoester, 2012). She also served as a consultant for the founding of several additional schools in New York City. I was hired as a teacher in a school in Boston in which she served as principal in the late 1990s and early 2000s. It was an eye-opening experience to see her interact with parents and families, since she was always interested in drawing families into the life of the school.

Meier was always deeply knowledgeable about the curriculum in the school and had well-thought-out ideas about how children learn. She hoped to share these ideas with parents, inviting them to take an interest and to ask their children about what they were learning. Parents were additionally invited to staff meetings, and a handful of them regularly attended (except when highly sensitive personnel issues were being discussed), including attending staff retreats, which took place three times per year. When the school hired for various positions in the school, including for teachers, teaching assistants, food service workers, security guards, office manager, or nurse, Meier almost always favored applicants who were parents of students in the school. This created a unique environment because whenever parents gathered together as part of the Family Council or other family gatherings, there were always school staff in attendance who could helpfully explain why particular decisions were made within the school. Likewise, whenever we had staff meetings, some of the staff members were also parents of children in the school, and they could speak as a parent about why one decision might be favored over another (Knoester, 2012).

Meier took the weekly newsletters of the school seriously and attempted to use this outlet not only to share important logistical information but to further explain the vision and mission of the school, connecting it to the curriculum, with lots of examples of real projects and activities within the school. It helped that she was an outstanding writer. The weekly newsletter included a column by the principal (about 500 words), but also mini-columns (about 150 words) by each of the teachers about what they were doing that week in the classroom. Lots of quotes and artwork from children were included. Parents could read a snapshot from their child's classroom teacher but could also gain a larger perspective about what was happening at the school from other teachers, and observe how the teachers worked together to plan lessons (generally all teaching within a large whole-school theme). Examples of newsletter columns written by Meier and two other well-known educational leaders, Ted and Nancy Sizer, were compiled in the book *Keeping School: Letters to Families From Principals of Two Small Schools* (2004). Here are a few truncated examples of columns Meier wrote to the school community in the weekly newsletter, published in the book:

On Snails

The first curriculum that the school got involved in happened by accident. Since we were starting a new school, we had thought that studying our neighborhood would be a good idea. We had lots of grandiose plans, and some of them got carried out. But, in fact, what really captured us all was the unexpected infestations of land snails we found everywhere around the schoolyard! There's never been anything like it since, so I don't know how to account for it. And then one thing led to another. It brought home an old truth: being interested is the starting point. It was a lucky accident of our history that land snails galore were as fascinating to five-year-olds as they were to sixty-five year-olds! (p. 15)

The Miracle of Reading for Pleasure

Book lovers have learned one special skill: to enjoy the adventures of other people, other times, and even other species, to thus add many lifetimes to our own. Too often, in the push for increased literacy, we focus on reading directions, or getting information—necessary, we claim, for success on the job (or in school). We too often ignore the power of a good story to expand our too-short lives tenfold—and not just in kindergarten. It's that ancient, fundamentally human love of a good story that is the biggest pedagogical tool we have for teaching reading. Like budding basketball players, a lover of reading can throw baskets morning, noon, and night. This was written as a plea for more reading-aloud at home and less worrying about when the child starts reading on his or her own. (pp. 17–18)

Tips for Parents

Try asking your kids different questions at home, like "Any interesting questions come up today at school?" "Did anyone say or do something surprising, odd, unusual, unexpected?" Or just tell *them* about what *you* learned that day—what interesting or surprising questions arose for you. Like "I had a different bus driver today because. . . ." Or "I figured out why Mr. So-and-so is always grumpy on Mondays. . . ." One thing sometimes leads to another. And here's a tip for parent conferences: Instead of "Was my child good today?" ask us "Did he surprise you today?" (p. 22)

In these short passages, it is possible to see descriptions of what students have been doing at school. Of course, these are just a taste of what happens. We can also notice that the tone of the letters is invitational. It asks parents to engage with their children about what they are experiencing at school. It also encourages families to read together, since we know that reading is something that accomplishes several tasks simultaneously: It can strengthen bonds among family members, it allows us to go deeper into areas in which we are already interested, it can be an enjoyable escape, and it can strengthen reading skills that are useful in school and for many other activities beyond school. Although newsletters can be characterized as "one-way" communication from school to home, they can also be based on information gathering from families and be encouraging to families who are looking for tips or insights into how to support their children.

ONE-WAY COMMUNICATION: GRADES AND REPORT CARDS

Grades on report cards are another way teachers communicate directly with parents. Different teachers and schools grade differently. Teachers generally offer points for students based on the work they complete doing various teacher-assigned tasks, although the specific tasks evaluated and the style of notation are likely to change, depending on the grade level of the child (e.g., using numbers or check marks at lower grades and letter grades and grade point averages for older students). These reports are important since learning is ultimately an apprenticeship between the student and the teacher, and it is important for parents and students to know how the teacher thinks the student is doing. A cautionary note: There is no one objective way to grade.

It is interesting to consider that schools have substantially different-looking report cards from one to another. This is a reminder that grades and report cards represent the specific priorities of the school and the teachers at that given time (report card formats can also change from year to year at the same school). Nevertheless, grades and report cards are valuable information because, for a parent, it is important to learn how the child is perceived by their teacher(s) in terms of effort and ability and what kind of rubric or descriptor teachers are using to assign grades and evaluations. Grades and report cards are also meant for multiple audiences—for both students and for parents. Teachers might want to send different messages to these two audiences, which can be tricky. For example, on the one hand, teachers might want to tell the student, "You can do better if you put in the effort." To the parent, the teacher might want to say, "I like this student and believe they have a lot of potential." Since report cards generally have a limited space for grades and comments, there is a good chance that both will be misinterpreted. There are significant limitations to what report cards can communicate.

As students grow older, their grades have higher stakes. Colleges and universities generally require a high school transcript as part of the application process. Selective colleges, and even high schools, will likely be more interested in accepting and perhaps providing financial aid to students who score higher on their report cards or transcripts. Despite the high stakes attached to grades and report cards at the higher levels, brevity is the point. Given the complexity of the task of evaluating learning, grades can therefore be a misleading indicator of student progress. Grades are a short and quick (often numeric) way for teachers to provide a general idea of how well each student is performing in the class, an assessment with both benefits and limitations. Parents are wise to pay attention to their children's grades and to encourage them to try their best, but they also should remember that their child is much more than a grade on a report card and that the child's strengths—such as, for example, kindness or empathetic attention to people different from themselves—may not even be measured or accurately represented by one grade or the accumulation of many grades.

Some report cards have larger boxes and space for teachers to make comments than do others. There are schools that have even done away with report cards altogether in favor of narrative reports for students. A more narrative approach can have significant advantages. For example, teachers can better tailor their messages to the specific students and families involved, making it clear to parents that the student is well-known by the teacher, carefully observed, and that the instruction is a good fit for the specific strengths and challenges of the student. A narrative report can more specifically describe the growth that students have demonstrated in a variety of areas, name particular achievements of students, describe student academic interests, and detail goals for the future. These are all valuable aspects of narrative report cards. There are downsides as well, of course. Narrative reports are time-consuming to write well, and teachers may be overwhelmed with the amount of work that writing such reports requires. So it is possible to see why hybrid report cards are sometimes preferred, those with both grades and text boxes. Nevertheless, narrative reports (and to a lesser extent, text boxes) offer an avenue to work around the miscommunication that is possible or perhaps likely with traditional report cards.

ONE-WAY COMMUNICATION: STANDARDIZED TEST SCORES

Another way schools communicate with parents is through the use of standardized test results. Standardized tests represent a way to see how students might compare to a grade-level standard and a way to understand what administrators and policymakers (those who create the test) most value and care about. The tests can only report a rough estimate about how a student is doing, which still can be helpful. However, we want to caution that we believe high-stakes standardized tests are overvalued and misused. In fact, these tests are quite inaccurate, given the scale on which they are used, and too often are misleading gauges of student learning, incentivizing harmful practices such as narrowing the curriculum to only tested subjects (Knoester & Au, 2017; Meier & Knoester, 2017).

There have been many criticisms of standardized tests made by various scholars, especially tests with high-stakes decisions attached to their results, such as decisions about students (like promotion or graduation), teachers (pay increases), administrators and schools (evaluations) that are directly tied to test scores. Contrary to the idea that they are a "snapshot" in time, they are not clear. They are at best a blurry snapshot. They are, by definition, quite inaccurate. This is because they can never measure the entire breadth of a student's knowledge, so with such a small sample, their conclusions can only be based on correlation and inference with a large margin of error. Further, and perhaps most concerning, they have been found to be biased based on race and class (Knoester & Au, 2017; Meier & Knoester, 2017; Nichols & Berliner, 2007). However, since they are bathed in the language of science and measurement, they are incorrectly viewed as "objective" and given more value than they merit.

We argue there are more effective assessments of student learning that support the central goal of educating for democratic citizenship, such as looking at authentic student work through the lens of a carefully designed rubric, portfolio presentations of student work, and other teacher- or school-designed assessments (Meier & Knoester, 2017). Quality assessment is a large topic that is beyond the scope of this book, and we recognize that standardized tests cannot be abandoned by schools due to school policy. We encourage parents to relay the message to their children to try their best on standardized tests but take test scores with a grain of salt, and remember that there are other, more accurate ways to monitor their child's progress in school. It is more important to focus on children's effort and engagement with school activities, carefully consider teachers' assessments and evaluations, and take in the assessment of multiple voices. If parents have serious concerns about their child's academic development—and concerns sometimes first arise with test scores—it may be necessary to ask for additional assessment from a school psychologist to verify results, which may lead to working with a specialist such as a special educator, speech and language therapist, occupational therapist, or tutor. Parents may want to consider additional tutoring or other kinds of assistance outside of the school. We will return to the subject of special education later in this chapter.

The real problem with high-stakes standardized tests are the "high stakes" involved. If standardized tests were used as information only but with no penalty for ignoring the results, there would not be such a large backlash against them. However, it is the high stakes tied to them that makes them dangerous and detrimental to education.

When the federal No Child Left Behind law was passed in 2002, it mandated that schools would be evaluated based on standardized test scores and that schools could be closed or taken over by the state if test scores did not consistently improve overall and in multiple subcategories over time. High school students were not allowed to graduate with a degree without passing the test. The goal of consistent improvement of test scores was called Adequate Yearly Progress (AYP). Even before it became clear that not a single school in the United States could maintain AYP year after year, the law lost popularity (despite its feel-good-sounding title). The law became unpopular, receiving greater disapproval than approval in public surveys, and it was not renewed with the same name in Congress. The law was significantly changed during the Obama administration and retitled the Every Student Succeeds Act. The new iteration included high-stakes standardized testing, but AYP was eliminated and the decisions about the consequences have been devolved to the state level. We continue to have serious concerns about high-stakes standardized tests, but they are becoming more properly understood as unworthy of having such enormous value placed on their scores, given their inaccuracies and biases.

ANOTHER CAUTIONARY NOTE ABOUT WRITTEN COMMUNICATIONS SENT HOME TO FAMILIES

In the aforementioned examples of one-way communications sent home to families from schools, important information can be shared, with varying quality of communication. However, we wish to caution that not only might families have limited time to review large amounts of information sent home from the school but that levels of literacy can vary widely among families.

Depending on the parent's level of education and where they come from, some families may not know how to read and write in English or perhaps in their native language. If parents are unable to read in English but can read in their native language, it is helpful if school newsletters, report cards, and standardized test scores are translated into that language. If these reports cannot be translated, or if parents are unable to read in any language, a different form of communication is necessary.

For example, I (Maura) once received a referral to work with a single mother from one of the schools with which I was consulting at the time. I will call her Mary. The school was having difficulty getting her to attend meetings, return signed consent forms, or respond to any notes the teachers sent home with her child. I visited Mary at her home after arranging the meeting by phone with her. Mary was welcoming and eager to talk about her child and looking to find ways to help him at home with schoolwork. I mentioned to her the school's concerns about communication, and she was very apologetic. She acknowledged receiving "papers" from the school and confessed that she had a very bad memory and was very forgetful. I asked her what would be the best and fastest way to receive information about school meetings, school events, or any information regarding her child. She immediately said it was better if the school would call her instead of sending pieces of papers. My antenna went up when she called the information from school "pieces of papers." I wondered if Mary could read and write. I had the dates and times for the upcoming school activities and provided them to Mary. I noticed she wasn't writing anything down. I like to write information about clients in notebooks, and I always carry extra. I offered her one of my notebooks and a pen. She was very appreciative of the notebook but asked me to write everything down for her. I have given her several dates and times for meetings and events at the school. I started to write down the information, and Mary was able to repeat every event, time, and place without missing a beat. She had memorized all the information as I had given it to her. I was impressed and realized that Mary had a very good memory. Her response to school meetings and events increased significantly, but the teachers were concerned again when the school had an early dismissal and she didn't show up to pick up her son. I didn't have this information in her notebook.

I visited Mary again several times, and each time I asked her to get the notebook I had given her. I wrote down everything for her once again. In one visit, I gave the notebook back and asked her to review the information I had given and realized that I had missed one of the events. I asked her to add it to the notebook under a date. She couldn't find the date or the information I had written down. I didn't know how to ask her about her literacy and decided to just ask. In a very respectful manner, I asked her if it was hard for her to read and write. She was defensive at first but finally told me she wasn't able. Mary was born and raised in the United States.

On relaying this story, the teachers became more intentional about communicating with parents and were able to share important school information by using the school's robocall system.

They became aware of the literacy factor and thought there may be other parents that were in the same predicament as Mary.

According to the National Literacy Institute (2025):

- Twenty-one percent of adults in the United States are illiterate in 2024.
- Fifty-four percent of adults have literacy below a 6th-grade level (20% are below a 5th-grade level).
- Fifty-four percent of adults read below a 6th-grade level.

Improving communication with parents may require schools to realize that some parents born in United States do not know how to read and write in English. Foreign nationals may be faced with the same challenge. Providing information orally and/or in different languages to connect with parents may be a solution.

TWO-WAY COMMUNICATION: PARENT–TEACHER CONFERENCES

Parent–teacher conferences have great potential to build a two-way relationship and communication. As we noted in the introduction, there are many ways for parents and teachers to miscommunicate or misunderstand one another as well, or to fail to arrive at a shared understanding. Most importantly, we believe, it is important for teachers to communicate that they know the child in focus, care about them, and have a plan for how to help the child move forward. These are broad goals, but they are essential elements. In order to be successful, deep knowledge is needed about the specific child, about child development, and about the subject matters that are part of the learning goals. The latter two sets of knowledge are generally learned outside of school, including in teacher preparation programs. But that first piece—knowledge about each individual child—requires powerful assessment that generally takes place within the school. The assessment can be based on close observations of the child, and listening to them, as they ask questions and respond to various challenges. The assessment can be based on looking at student work, including daily classwork, artwork, homework, tests, and quizzes. It can also be based on asking the child questions and carrying on interactions. It can be based as well on talking with various colleagues who have worked with and observed the student.

Another powerful source of information about children is their parents and family members. In order to learn from parents, teachers must listen. Parent–teacher conferences are prime opportunities to do this if the teacher uses the time wisely. Come prepared with questions and carve out time to make sure the teacher does not do all the talking. Of course, these are also opportunities for teachers to ask questions of the parents about anything the parent might want to know about and to explain anything parents don't understand, which might involve dispelling myths. Berger and Riojas-Cortez (2016) offer these reminders about parent–teacher conferences:

> Show respect for the parents, give total attention to the parents, use culturally appropriate communication, listen and restate the parents' concerns, recognize parents' feelings, tailor discussions to fit the parents' ability to handle the situation, do not set off the fuse of a parent who might not be able to handle a child's difficulties, emphasize that concerns are no one's fault, remember that no one ever wins an argument, focus on one issue at a time, tackle barriers when working with a parents with a disability, become allies with parents. (pp. 131–132)

Although this passage was written with educators as the main audience in mind, these recommendations could be helpful for parents as well. Using these skills may create a more productive working relationship with educators and may also be more effective in gaining the information a parent seeks.

Aside from the logistical issue of finding a time to meet, a central challenge with parent–teacher conferences is that they are often too short (15 minutes is not enough time to say much substantively). Given the time constraints, they often feature the teacher reporting why a student received the grade they did. In our view, a very short conference offers little more than the report card itself.

A more powerful format is a bit longer, at least 30 minutes, with enough time for each party to speak and learn from one another. Conferences can be even more effective with the focal student involved, perhaps leading the discussion of what they are learning in school (perhaps prepared with the teacher beforehand) and the teacher asking the parents questions. This can be significant, since it provides a space for students to be heard and for their viewpoint to be included and valued, but it is also an opportunity for parents and teachers to speak with "one voice" to the child, demonstrating that they are working together as a team. Students can demonstrate their knowledge and interests in these settings, providing a real-time assessment for adults to notice more about the child and their engagement in school. It might not be appropriate to involve the student in certain cases in which sensitive information might be discussed. For example, in the next section we turn to IEP (Individualized Education Program) meetings.

TWO-WAY COMMUNICATION: INDIVIDUALIZED EDUCATION PROGRAM (IEPs) AND 504 PLANS

Throughout this book, we have discussed integration and inclusion, focusing mostly on race and ethnicity, immigration, and class status. In this section, we discuss inclusion in the sense of (dis)abilities. The rights of students (and adults) with disabilities have come a long way. This is wonderful progress. In the not-too-distant "bad old days," the response by schools to students with disabilities was seclusion. Fortunately, the movement(s) that have centered special education have been bipartisan, and the strongest federal laws that support the inclusion of people with special education, such as the Individuals with Disabilities Education Act (IDEA) of 1975 and its reauthorization in 2004, were passed during Republican presidential administrations and with bipartisan Congressional support.

Parents have been at the forefront of this movement. They have advocated for their own children and for other children with disabilities. The rights of students with disabilities are powerful and have substantial federal resources attached to them. Therefore, IEPs and 504 plans are critically important. These meetings are more than parent–teacher conferences, which, as discussed earlier in this chapter, are informational and provide an opportunity for parents and teachers to communicate with one another and to work together. IEP meetings, which are required to be held annually with regard to a student with an identified disability, must include not only a parent and teacher but also specialists that work with the child and a representative of the school district. The document they create, the IEP, is also a legally binding document. When schools are reluctant to or do not provide adequate resources for students with disabilities, these resources can be obtained through the judicial process. So, it is important that parents of students with disabilities speak up, attend meetings, and advocate for their child.

Under federal law, students with disabilities have the right to be educated within the "least restrictive environment" (LEA), which generally means included in mainstream schools with accommodations such as assistive technologies or specialists that can help these students to be successful. Depending on the student's disability(ies), the IEP team (including the parents) may decide that working in a separate classroom for part or all of the day is more appropriate. There are many other rights that parents and students with disabilities enjoy. For example, parents have the right to attend the annual IEP meetings concerning their child and to consent or withhold consent from the IEP document that specifies the provision of accommodations for their child. Parents have the right to bring other adults who know the child to the IEP meeting. They have the right to insist the IEP meeting be held after school or after working hours. They also have the right to insist that the special educator and general education teacher attend the meeting (Wright et al., 2015).

Mainstream students also benefit from being educated with students with disabilities. Some parents, educators, and students need to be reminded that people with disabilities are important contributors to the larger society, and all students (and adults) need to learn to include people with disabilities in more, if not all, spaces. In fact, it may be useful to remember that nearly all of us will have a disability at some point in our lives—whether the condition is temporary or permanent. We all want to be included, and seeing people with disabilities as part of "us" is the reframing that is necessary. Parents and schools should continually ask themselves, "How can we become a more inclusive community?" "How can I teach my child to think about the inclusion of others?" This is part of the ongoing work of a democratic school.

TWO-WAY COMMUNICATION: FAMILY NIGHTS

Schools often find that family attendance at school events is highest when students are performing or showcasing their work or their abilities. For example, if students are performing music, theater, dance, sports, or presenting their artwork or writing, or some combination of the above, these are strong reasons for parents to attend the event and support their children. Events such as these, which might be called "family nights" and may also include food or other attractive activities, are prime opportunities for schools and families to communicate with one another.

Events that include any of the activities listed above can be considered part of the curriculum. During family nights, schools are sending messages and parents can make inferences about what they are noticing about the students' and school's work and the activities involved. This is a powerful form of communication. What does the student work show? What are the major themes? What are the messages being sent to both the students and the families about what is valued and prioritized by the school? These types of questions are carefully considered by educators as they plan for the family night. Family nights can also be good opportunities for teachers and administrators to directly address families with explicit messages, such as directly welcoming them to the event with an opening statement, and which might emphasize an aspect of the mission of the school and its curriculum.

On the other hand, schools can also seize the opportunity to use these kinds of events to listen to the thoughts and experiences of families. Informal conversations might take place for educators to hear from families. If families who attend the event perhaps missed the most recent parent–teacher conferences or haven't returned paperwork or surveys, the family night might be a prime opportunity for an educator or administrator to connect with them. For a more comprehensive approach at gathering information from families, the school might send out surveys to families before the family night and use the event to follow up on the survey, reminding families to fill out the survey, or even to conduct the survey orally with families, if that might be the best way to collect information. This approach is more comprehensive because the school might hear from more families and ask questions that families might need more time to think about and to answer, as opposed to a parent–teacher conference, a meeting of a governance board, or other meeting-like gathering.

One of the schools in which I (Matthew) taught hosted a family night nearly every month. These events were very well attended by families and always included some kind of student performance or display, along with food. During these events, I was able to have the greatest number of informal conversations with families as compared to any other time. Families seemed most likely to bring up questions or concerns during these times. The family nights at our school were designed to allow this to happen, with a portion of the event "all together" as a school and a portion of the time spent within the classrooms, as families came in and out of various classrooms to see the student work that was showcased and to have an informal conversation with the teacher.

TWO-WAY COMMUNICATION: BOOK STUDY DISCUSSIONS

With effective communication about ongoing curricula, families can better understand the experiences of their children and support and enhance their child's learning. For difficult conversations, parent–teacher conferences, or carefully planned meetings outside of regular conferences are beneficial, as well as ongoing discussion. There are also issues in education that may not be directly connected with one's own child but that merit inquiry and study by parents and educators alike. We suggest book clubs as one example of how to come to a deeper understanding of different cultural values around sensitive topics and how all students, parents, and educators can be treated with dignity and respect.

A key reason we wrote this book is because it is worth considering deeply the complex dynamics and inequalities that take place within schools and within the interactions between parents, educators, and students. Building trust and productive communication in schools is a delicate dance. We know that many (not all) parents yearn to know more about schools, and perhaps most importantly, how parents can support their children academically and socially. We also know that many educators yearn to know more about parents and what is happening at home for their students. There are perhaps too many assumptions that are made about one another, often incorrectly. This book is a way toward beginning or deepening that conversation, toward building greater understanding based on communication and listening to one another, not based on false assumptions.

Earlier in this chapter, we wrote about Deborah Meier and the school in which one of us taught along with her. This school community included several parents that seemed to always want to know more about the school and how decisions were made. They attended staff meetings and even staff retreats. Some served on the Family Council and volunteered in the school. Some joined a book club that included both parents and teachers, meeting once per month (we called the group "First Tuesdays"). For some of these parents, education was an abiding interest. They had perhaps taken an education class at a university and were already familiar with books and key concepts associated with teaching. Other parents had not read a single book about education but wanted to better understand how they might support their child's learning.

Parents and educators might want to discuss issues of multicultural education. There are many other topics that parents may want to know more about and can learn just by having discussions with other parents. Parents can certainly learn a lot from other parents, and schools might be places where they can come together to learn from one another. The topics parents want to discuss might not even be directly related to school. Such topics include bedtimes or nighttime routines, meal times, healthy eating, negotiating expectations, chores, friendships, play dates, transportation, best deals for merchandise, services that may be available for families, family dynamics, marriages or dating, gender roles, how to encourage reading, how to manage screen time with children, manners and etiquette, being social and creating social opportunities for kids, to name a few. These subjects are not likely to arise and be seriously considered in most of the forms of communication discussed in this chapter, although book clubs and family nights might be situations in which such discussions can begin, or relationships made, that can lead to deeper discussion in another setting.

CONCLUSION

This chapter has focused on just some of the many ways that schools and parents can communicate in order to better collaborate on the education of children. There are many other possible ways to communicate. In addition to the forms of communication we included in this chapter, Berger and Riojas-Cortez (2016) offer this list of additional forms of communication: student-written periodic newsletters, personalized notes, suggestion boxes, handbooks, summer handbook, homework hotline, email, chats, phone calls, visits to the classroom, visits by invitation, student–parent exchange day, and breakfasts.

In their chapter aptly titled "Developing Relationships: How Can You Build Trust Instead of Blaming Each Other?" Henderson et al. (2007) offer helpful tips about communication:

> People listen genuinely to each other, parents can talk with teachers and feel they have a say in what happens to their children, teachers can voice their concerns, people's words and actions are consistent, teachers stay after hours to meet with parents, school staff get involved in local community matters. (pp. 50–79)

They further offer ideas for higher family turnout at school events:

> Send[ing] handwritten notes home, inviting families to teach a lesson, join[ing] their children for a BBQ lunch, plant[ing] a class garden, [being] on a first-name basis with all of the students' parents, mak[ing] sure each parent has her cell phone number, honor[ing] families by recognizing their strengths and contributions, adopt[ing] a partnership philosophy, [not being] afraid to ask parents for help or advice, [not] hesitat[ing] to apologize, and listen[ing] and respond[ing] to families. (pp. 50–79)

These suggestions illustrate that trust and quality communication is based on relationship-building, which requires thoughtful intention. It is a lot to ask of overworked teachers. If anything, perhaps it is most important that schools avoid actions that send messages to families such as:

> [Asking visitors] "Who are you? What do you want?" [posting] no trespassing signs, parent officers dominating parent meetings, large meetings in the school gym, meeting only during school hours, and "announcing" a new reading program (as opposed to asking for guidance). (p. 59)

There are many ways to enhance family involvement and collaboration in schools and to build a stronger community. The ideas included in this chapter have worked well in some communities; other school communities may need something different. Schools cannot offer all things to all people. But school personnel and families can work together to identify the forms of communication that work best for their specific communities.

Still, despite all of these strategies, we want to caution that great communication may still not be enough to build trust among parents and teachers. In the next chapter, we turn to some of the most challenging aspects of building trust in school communities.

DISCUSSION QUESTIONS

1. What might be an example in which a school with which you are familiar communicated very well? How would you describe the communication?
2. What are the most inclusive ways to communicate? How might communication be differentiated for different families' needs and preferences?
3. For both parents and teachers: How often do you think parent–teacher or family conferences should be held, and how long should each meeting be? What are the specific topics you would like to be discussed?
4. During parent–teacher or family conferences, does it make sense for the teacher to do most of the talking, the parent, or about 50/50?
5. What should teachers be hearing about from parents during parent–teacher conferences?
6. What do you think should be the role of the student, if any, in a parent–teacher conference?

7. Are the report cards that are sent home clear to the parent? Is there anything you wish was changed or included in the report card?
8. For teachers: What might be effective ways to communicate with parents who may not know how to read and write at a high enough level to make sense of report cards and newsletters?

CHAPTER 5

The Most Challenging Aspects of Building Trust

> Never has it been more important that we learn how to relate to people we don't automatically trust, who aren't kin or otherwise obvious allies, but strangers we must deal with "as if" we trusted each other, as if being human itself was grounds for respect.
>
> —Deborah Meier (2002, p. 179)

In this chapter, we turn to some of the most challenging aspects of building trust between parents and educators. In the previous chapters, we focused on high-quality communication, collaboration, and partnerships between families and educators, which are not easy to achieve but are worthy goals that can ultimately provide better opportunities for student learning. In order to achieve these kinds of relationships, building trust is essential. Students are strongly affected by both home and school when they work together. If home and school are sending the same or similar messages to students, this unity and shared purpose can supercharge their educational progress. But even excellent communication is not enough to build trust when schools and parents are fundamentally at odds on priorities. In this chapter, we describe (and encourage discussion about) challenging and sometimes controversial topics like discipline and homework, and how implicit cultural bias and prejudice can present itself in school decisions and activities.

Deborah Meier (2002) reminds us that democracy itself requires trust. She writes:

> Modern democratic and pluralistic societies require trust even when their members are, in fact, very different from each other. We

> need to be able to count on each other most of the time to act "as if" we were trustworthy, even as we also know that we will often enough have our trust betrayed. (pp. 179–180)

Why is this quote from Meier true? One reason is that in a democracy, we need to believe that our elections are fair and legitimate, for example, and that we can live with the results. Otherwise, people might disregard the government as illegitimate, making it courageous to denounce and disobey laws. This does not mean we are saying "just trust," blindly, when authorities or public institutions have not earned our trust. Critically analyzing and verifying election results and other governmental actions, for example, is important. A free and proactive press is fundamental when seeking accountability from our political leaders, and a free press is often the first to go in a dictatorship. Repair and remediation for misdeeds must follow, not only rhetorically. Gaining public trust is essential to a functioning democracy that depends on shared governance.

Likewise, trust is essential to classrooms and schools as well. Teachers need to build trust with students for nearly the same reasons outlined above. After all, teachers are far outnumbered by students, so they must build trust with their students in order to create a functional learning environment in which students willingly accept their guidance. Further, parents, who outnumber teachers by even greater numbers than students, need to trust teachers and schools that they are taking good care of their children.

Unfortunately, schools face an uphill battle building trust in many parts of the United States. This is in part because trust is a collective endeavor, and the United States can be fairly characterized as a society that values individualism. For example, each year a poll is carried out by Kappan/Gallup polls, and parents consistently report approval of the school of their child but not of the nation's schools (see the 54th annual PDK poll at https://pdkpoll.org/2022-pdk-poll-results/). Survey results such as this suggest that while parents may have a higher level of trust in a school with which they have a direct relationship and personal knowledge, they are swayed by a national narrative that "schools are failing." Mistrust between parents and the school their children attend can result for many reasons. In the following sections, we turn to some of the major issues that are known to be sites of conflict within schools.

HOMEWORK

Homework is an example of a sometimes-controversial topic in education, since it requires coordination between home and school. The right amount of homework can work well, be received gladly by families, and help students grow academically. But a large number of elements need to go right for that to work. Many teachers and parents see homework as expanding on what the student is learning in school. Based on the idea that learning complex concepts and tasks requires practice, teachers would ideally assign something that a student would not resist, makes sense, and extends a student's understanding and skill. It helps if a parent echoes what a teacher says (or writes) about it, does not undermine or talk badly about the work or the teacher who assigned it, and provides the student with encouragement and a quiet place to work and creates a routine that is sustainable. Homework may be beneficial, especially if the parent and teacher have significant concerns about a child's reading or math level and wishes for additional support.

However, there are many potential drawbacks with homework as well. These drawbacks are worsened with miscommunication and nonalignment between the school and parents about the conditions necessary for a child to succeed. For example, if a child is very busy with transportation, family responsibilities, other activities, or does not have an adult around to encourage or check on them, it is unlikely the homework will get done. If the parent does not support the idea of homework or if they feel they need to fight with the child to have them do the homework, it is probably a losing battle over time that has more negative aspects than positive. If for whatever reason homework increases tension in the relationships at home, it may be causing more harm than good.

Teachers could try to differentiate each child's homework, but this requires accurate understanding of children's needs and home situations. There are likely misunderstandings on the part of the teacher about the ways the homework is interpreted at home. Another of the key dangers with homework is that if students are not keeping up with it, it is tempting for teachers to blame parents and assume they "do not care about their child's education." This is not helpful. On the flip side, if teachers assign homework that is simple or requires a low level of critical thinking, parents may incorrectly assume the homework is representative of the entire curriculum. Homework in these conditions is not so important that it merits the risk of raising these tensions and the potential of fomenting distrustful relationships between teachers and parents.

At one of the schools in which I (Matthew) taught, in order to simplify homework, we agreed as a school that our main suggestion would be that students should read at home independently, with an adult or with a sibling for approximately a half-hour every day. The thought was that research has found this activity beneficial to children and also can lead to closer relationships between people who read together. Whether done just before bed or at another time, it provides an opportunity for quality time together, for the child to step into an imaginary world, a time to talk about various subjects, and helps a child fall asleep at a reasonable hour. Granted, not every parent has the energy, ability, or interest to read with their child every night (or to regularly check out books from the library or purchase new books), but reading together is quality time with few downsides.

As a teacher of 9–11-year-olds, I asked students to write in a journal once per week about what they read. I wrote a response to each student, continuing a dialog with them about books and reading, which taught me a lot. My daughter's 3rd-grade teacher did something similar, which I greatly appreciated. I wanted my daughter to be reading and writing more; both activities, I thought, supported the growth of her reading, spelling, and comprehension. I loved working as a "tag team" with my daughter's teacher to make sure this was done on time, and my daughter barely resisted this reasonable expectation, which was supported at home and at school.

In any case, making a quality decision about homework—whether it is better to assign homework or not, and whether to differentiate it based on knowledge of how students respond to the assignment—depends on high-quality communication between the school and family. Teachers are wise to further assume that parents care deeply about their children's education, even if a child's homework is not getting done.

DISCIPLINE

Another topic that often leads to miscommunication and distrust is student discipline. While maintaining student discipline in schools is mostly about setting and communicating clear and reasonable expectations and consistently enforcing them, we estimate that discipline is the topic most likely to expose cultural conflict. In fact, we have noticed that discussing discipline is often avoided due to its potential to expose tensions. Parents can have dramatically different views on discipline, which are often culturally situated, informed, and identified. Some parents may expect teachers to be very strict, for example, to reflect their parenting style. Others may expect teachers to be gentler and more informal to reflect their parenting style. There can also be different discipline styles/abilities/philosophies among different teachers.

After conducting research on this topic, Milner et al. (2019) found:

> "These kids are out of control" is a statement we often hear. With the best of intentions, teachers often believe they should be able to "control" students in the classroom and broader school community.

Milner et al. focused their book on trying to disrupt this discourse about school discipline. They write:

> But a central goal of this book project is to disrupt such thinking because students are developing human beings, and our goal should not be to attempt to control them or their behaviors. Teachers should be vigilant in their efforts to co-create a classroom environment that is safe, affirming, learning centered, innovative, intellectually challenging, and engaging. Rather than attempting to control students, teachers must work to maximize students' opportunities to learn in order to enhance their academic and social development. Students rightfully resist adults' efforts to control them. (p. 1)

It is hard to argue with a statement like this. But as the saying goes, "perception is reality," and students and parents can often perceive teachers and administrators as trying to "control" their children. And worse, parents may perceive teachers as not treating their child as well as they are treating other children, in terms of enforcement of rules and expectations. Distrust can grow.

Allow me (Hervé) to share a personal example of a conflict between my own family and the school regarding one of my children. When my daughter was in middle school, she chose to participate in an extracurricular activity: skiing. The fee for participating was $300, already an exclusionary fee for students with families on a tight budget. Before the start of the season, the assistant principal called her into her office and asked whether she would feel comfortable skiing along with an almost entirely White team. My daughter said yes. The ski resort was located 30 miles away from the school, and students were to be transported by school bus. A couple of weeks after the season started, the assistant principal, who was also chaperoning the trip, sent home a note to us to the effect that my daughter could no longer participate in the activity because she was late to the bus on their way back home. The assistant principal enjoined us to send the remainder of the $100 due (as we had already paid $200). Again, I found myself obliged to intervene and called the school. I told the school principal that if there was any issue, the channels of communication between school and home should be open enough and that I suspected from the beginning that the school begrudgingly accepted my daughter into the program. I mentioned that the question asked of my daughter before the program started was inappropriate. The principal apologized and said that she would not allow discrimination of students on the basis of race or any other factor.

This may seem like an insignificant example of a disagreement between parents and school, but it serves to highlight that disciplinary issues can often have cultural and racial aspects. While school staff might believe that they are following a "colorblind" set of rules, there are almost always unconscious biases at work, or perceived biases. Distrust can quickly grow.

I (Maura) offer here another example of contradictory understandings about student behavior, relating to my own daughter. In fact, there were several incidents in which my daughter—who, I admit, was not always a perfect angel—was accused of initiating trouble at school, sometimes even if she wasn't at school on the day in question (which raised my suspicions about the truth of the claims). I believe my daughter was the first Latina student for several of her teachers, and that may have been part of why she was sometimes accused. One day, when my daughter was in 4th grade, my husband and I were asked to meet with one of her teachers. At the meeting, the teacher informed us that our daughter was "out of control" and would often get out of her seat during class without asking permission. The teacher suggested that our daughter may need medication. The teacher did not provide an explanation for this suggestion, but we interpreted it to mean she thought our daughter should be tested for attention deficit hyperactivity disorder (ADHD).

Our daughter was high energy and loved sports from an early age. She was also an avid reader, and after doing her homework and having dinner, she would go to her room to read just about every day. Sometimes we would find her reading with a flashlight under her covers when she was supposed to be asleep. My husband and I were therefore surprised about the teacher's recommendation for our daughter and asked permission of the teacher to have one of our friends, who was a child psychologist, observe our daughter in the classroom. The principal and the teacher agreed with our request.

Our daughter was observed in class for several days. Our friend then met with our daughter one-on-one. After concluding her evaluation, the friend met with us. She told us she observed and noticed that our daughter frequently got out of her seat once she had completed her assignment/s and would regularly walk around the room helping other students with their assignments. She added that our daughter was never disruptive. She further noticed that the teacher never asked our daughter to go back to her seat during the observations. Our friend did not know whether the teacher was not asking our daughter to sit down because a psychologist was observing her, and perhaps the teacher responded differently without an observer present.

The psychologist's report provided insightful information. In her session with our daughter, she learned that our daughter thought she was helping the teacher. Our daughter also confessed that she was bored doing nothing after completing her work.

Our friend did not feel that our daughter needed any medication. We spoke with our daughter about classroom rules and helped her understand how important it was to respect her teachers.

My husband and I shared the report with the teacher and offered a suggestion. The teacher was open to ideas. We reminded her how much our daughter loved to read. We suggested that the teacher provide a table or a designated reading area for all the students. The teacher liked the idea and was willing to give it a try. She then spoke to our daughter one-on-one about classroom rules and acceptable behavior. It turns out the reading corner was an instant hit, and we believe it is still in use at the school. Our daughter was rewarded with reading time, along with other students who completed their assignments early.

In the end, my husband and I felt heard by the teacher due to her willingness to work with us to find a solution as a team. The result created a sense of trust and partnership that we did not previously enjoy. Although we believe the teacher had misunderstood the needs of our daughter, we were able to work together to improve our daughter's experience, as well as the orderly functioning of the classroom in the eyes of the teacher.

We realize this was a specific case, and not everyone has a friend who is a child psychologist who can help the family and teacher resolve differences. Ideally, parents can build trust with the school staff directly, including perhaps with the school's psychologist. We also know there are additional tools and assessments available that can enable teachers, parents, and other school personnel to work together to reach deeper and more holistic understandings of students (Himley & Carini, 2000; Meier & Knoester, 2017). One such method is called the Descriptive Review of the Child, described on this website: https://www.clee.org/resources/descriptive-review-of-a-child/.

The Descriptive Review of the Child process is a shared inquiry, using a framing question having to do with a specific child. In the preceding case, with Maura's daughter, the framing question might be, "How can I support this child and also maintain order in the classroom?" The teacher leads the inquiry, and before gathering colleagues and sometimes the parents of the child together, the teacher first carefully observes and answers a large number of specific questions about the child (listed on the aforementioned website). The teacher is asked to describe what she sees of the child in various settings and not to diagnose or to label the child. During the meeting, the teacher shares what she wrote. This is followed by steps that include other participants' descriptions, clarifying questions, probing questions, and suggestions for the teacher. The teacher responds to each of these or can merely listen. The purpose of the process is to be more descriptive and holistic about the child and then to brainstorm as a group ways or teaching strategies that might support the child, the teacher, and perhaps others in the classroom. The downside of the process is that it is time consuming. However, the benefits of such a process are significant in that very challenging questions about children and group dynamics can be better and more intentionally addressed with a group effort, organized around a carefully crafted set of questions and procedures.

To summarize this section, we focused here on the significant challenges of thoughtful student discipline within schools and the potential for miscommunication and mistrust to take root between schools and families around these issues. We offered two personal examples of mistrust developing between parents and educators, with different resolutions (one more positive than the other). We also offered a short description of a promising assessment process that educators could use, the Descriptive Review of the Child, which has been found to offer deeper understandings of students, including around issues affecting relationships and discipline in schools. Other resources that may be helpful to educators include *Teaching Children to Care* by Ruth Charney (2002) and, for parents, *No Drama Discipline* by Daniel J. Siefel and Tina Payne Bryson (2016).

THE CHALLENGE OF SENDING MIXED MESSAGES TO PARENTS

Another obstacle to building trust between parents and educators has to do with sending a consistent message to parents. At the beginning of the previous chapter on communication, we suggested that communication involves coalescing around a shared vision for the school. If the vision is well-thought-out, all of the ensuing communication should be aligned with the vision. However, communication may unintentionally be sending mixed or contradictory messages either because different people are saying (and believing) contradictory things or are perhaps unknowingly sending mixed messages due to unclear communication.

Following extensive ethnographic work with families and schools, Lareau (2011) reported the following exchange between a teacher and a parent:

> During [a] parent–teacher conference, Mr. Tier, Wendy's fourth-grade teacher, expresses his outrage that [Wendy] has made it to fourth grade without knowing how to read. He urges Ms. Driver [Wendy's mother] to be more demanding with him and other school personnel, telling Ms. Driver in a parent–teacher conference: "If our roles were reversed—I'd be beating me on the head." Here, Mr. Tier suggests that Ms. Driver should take a concerted cultivation approach to her daughter's education. She should aggressively monitor, criticize, and even badger educators rather than simply following the professionals' advice. He shifts much of the responsibility for Wendy's current predicament away from these expert decision makers and on to her mother, implying that had Ms. Driver taken this approach from the start, Wendy's reading deficiency would never have been "allowed" to persist. (p. 211)

As this example suggests, schools may be sending mixed messages to parents. On the one hand, schools send the message that families should trust the school to educate their child, to assess and monitor the child's progress fairly, and to make appropriate teaching adjustments accordingly. But on the other hand, the message is sent—such as in the preceding example—that the parent should advocate for their child within the school (for special education services or other interventions, for example). It can be confusing! The truth is that both of these messages could be true at different times when dealing with the complex and challenging task of educating a child who is struggling. Contradictory statements might be inevitable if an adequate solution to a child's difficulties remains unidentified or if progress is slow.

However, given the confusion that can result from mixed messages from the school to the parents, and the possibility that mixed messages might undermine trust between them, it is worthwhile for school personnel to continually reflect on the possible ways mixed messages might be getting sent and how schools can send clearer and more coherent and supportive messages to families through their various forms of communication.

UNEQUAL VOICE FOR PARENTS WITHIN SCHOOLS

Researchers have described another unfortunate form of inequality that takes place in schools with clear implications for parents (Ishimaru, 2019). Scholars have found that even in diverse public schools, a pattern of entitlement on the part of middle-class White parents often exists. Researchers caution that sharing space and resources among people with different cultural assumptions, expectations, economic resources, and ways of communicating can endanger the goal of interrupting the reproduction of inequality. For example, Howard (2016) argued that dominant groups, such as White middle-class parents, are often not even aware of their privilege and entitlement: "Dominant groups tend to claim truth as their private domain. . . . As [W]hites, we usually don't even think of ourselves as having culture; we're simply 'right.' Dominant groups don't hold 'perspectives.' They hold 'truth'" (p. 30). This assumption can cause problems when a group of diverse parents work together to deliberate and make decisions about school issues, such as within groups like a parent–teacher organization (PTO) or on a school-based governing board.

Posey-Maddox (2014) conducted extensive ethnographic research focusing on parental involvement in a diverse public school and found that "middle–class parents often intervene in ways that benefit their own children" (p. 4). This can mean advocating for curricular programs or resources that uniquely benefit their children and their interests, while marginalizing or ignoring the interests and priorities of working-class families. Similarly, Horvat et al. (2003) found that "middle-class parents, largely as a result of their network ties, have considerably greater resources at their disposal . . . than their working-class and poor counterparts" (p. 327). This can mean that these parents have a greater say over what happens as a matter of school policies or practices. Posey-Maddox (2014) lamented this difference in parental power in schools, not only because different parents have different amounts of influence, but because of the fundraising capabilities of middle-class and wealthy parents, schools can become too dependent on these parents. Posey-Maddox wrote, "relying on middle class [families] to fill gaps in public dollars . . . unfairly positions parents as the primary drivers of school improvement . . . [and] absolves [the] state of responsibility" (p. 5). It is more equitable to demand that schools be fairly funded at the district and state level and that all parents be given equal and adequate voice in school affairs. Changes demanded by middle-class parents can happen swiftly, according to Horvat et al. (2003), who found that "[middle-class] parents' ties to other parents often enabled them to . . . descend on the school en masse" (p. 331), including demanding a change of leadership of the school or even of individual teachers. We will return to this question in the next chapter.

Mindful of this research, we encourage parents to ask themselves, "How can I avoid using and abusing a sense of entitlement in an integrated school?" In a school that educates for democracy, we would hope all members of the school community are given free and fair opportunities to have their voices heard and to show respect and deference to the needs and preferences of all parents, even as they may differ from our own.

CONFRONTING RACE AND RACISM IN SCHOOLS

Great communication may still not be enough to build trust among parents and teachers. Some parents will not read school newsletters, for example, will not show up for family events or conferences, will not agree with school decisions, will have unreasonable demands, or will show denial of the limitations (financial or otherwise) of the school. There may be understandable reasons for any of these reactions. Some parents may also become exhausted by others' ignorance (especially if tinged with racism), resistance, or disrespect, leading them to avoid participating, compounded by the feeling of being overwhelmed with work or other responsibilities in life. Some parents may be genuinely confused about the differences between ethnocentrism (the idea that their culturally specific knowledge, culture, or preferences are inherently better than others) and academic knowledge, which is accepted within the curricular standards of the school district.

Willful ignorance is a problem. We all have heard the phrase, "ignorance is bliss." Ignorance may be blissful for the ignorant, but it can have negative effects for those around them (and, of course, we are all ignorant to a certain degree). Without knowledge of sociology, grown adults say things like "I didn't know that was offensive!" after making a statement based on a negative stereotype, or "I never thought about that!" We know from both research and personal experiences that statements and interactions reflecting negative stereotypes, sometimes called "microaggressions," take place on a daily basis (DiAngelo, 2018; Kendi, 2016).

It is hard for school communities to counteract dominant narratives found in the media and elsewhere that demean marginalized communities. For example, in recent years, there has been harsh language used toward immigrants, including by politicians at the highest levels. Negative stereotypes about immigrants are not new. Consider the negative stereotype "Mexicans are lazy." Those of us who are old enough may remember the popular cartoon *Speedy Gonzalez,* which included depictions of lazy Mexicans, with the exception of the title character, Speedy Gonzalez. The stereotype targets real-life Mexicans and places blame for social problems on the "laziness" of Mexicans. However, what this cheap stereotype reveals is the fundamental misunderstanding of those holding it. It shows deep ignorance. What this ignorance, at the same time, allows is a feeling of entitlement—that people "like them" (White viewers) deserve the opportunities, wealth, and experiences they have received. We all have received countless negative stereotypical depictions of various cultural groups via the media we have consumed (Ward & Bridgewater, 2023). We all remain on a learning curve to combat these depictions, but we can continually improve our critical thinking with effort, including reading, discussing, exposing ourselves to new experiences, and engaging in critical self-reflection.

In previous chapters, we began to discuss the problem of resistance to discussing race, racism, and harmful unconscious or conscious biases, even when these phenomena may be substantial obstacles to respectful dialogue in schools. In her work to build trust across racial divides, Robin DiAngelo (2018), a White woman, describes what she calls "White fragility," or a resistance of White people to talk about and acknowledge when racism is present. This resistance can arise even among teachers who are required as part of their job to undergo diversity training. DiAngelo writes:

> In the early days of my work as what was then termed a diversity trainer, I was taken aback by how angry and defensive so many [W]hite people became at the suggestion that they were connected to racism in any way. The very idea that they would be required to attend a workshop on racism outraged them. They entered the room angry and made that feeling clear to us throughout the day as they slammed their notebooks down on the table, refused to participate in exercises, and argued against any and all points.
>
> It took me several years to see beneath these reactions. At first, I was intimidated by them, and they held me back and kept me careful and quiet. But over time, I began to see what lay beneath this anger and resistance to discuss race or listen to people of color. I observed consistent responses from a variety of participants.
>
> I began to see what I think are the pillars of [W]hiteness—the unexamined beliefs that prop up our racial responses. I could see the power of the belief that only bad people were racist, as well as how individualism allowed [W]hite people to exempt themselves from the forces of socialization. I could see how we are taught to think about racism only as discrete acts committed by individual people, rather than as a complex, interconnected system. And in light of so many [W]hite expressions of resentment toward people of color, I realized that we see ourselves as entitled to, and deserving of, more than people of color deserve; I saw our investment in a system that serves us. I also saw how hard we worked to deny all this and how defensive we became when these dynamics were named. In turn, I saw how our defensiveness maintained the racial status quo. (pp. 2–4)

I (Maura) have seen these same antics in my work, including with educators and school personnel. Allow me to build on the thoughts of DiAngelo just quoted. In my work as a DEIB consultant, I have discovered something similar, which I have called the racial discomfort principle. As a DEIB practitioner, I always want to find root causes of racism and discrimination, due to their negative impacts on building trust within diverse communities. For instance, as a woman of color, I wanted to understand why people didn't seem to see me. This phenomenon has occurred to me not only in the United States but when I travel internationally. I discovered that racial discomfort impacts what we see, hear, who we associate with, and how we treat, serve, work, or deal with others.

I believe that racial discomfort (there are other types of discomfort such as disabilities, gender, lifestyles, etc., but for the purpose of this book I am going to write about racial discomfort only) makes us think we are unable to see, communicate, approach, deal with, or serve others who may be perceived differently from us to eliminate discomfort.

Below are examples of reactions I have noticed, perhaps due to racial discomfort or lack of exposure (racial discomfort uses what is unfamiliar or discomfort as a defense mechanism):

1. Not able to see a person at all
2. Turning on the primitive alert mode—fight or flight, depending on where we are and with whom
3. Making us walk away and terminate an interaction
4. Making us disregard/ignore a person(s) or situation altogether
5. Making us ignore the value of another person—thinking of the person as less than
6. Ignoring the other person's contributions

The higher the level of racial discomfort a person feels, the more critical that person may become of a person perceived as different. Hence, poor performance reviews, declined advancements, excessively high expectations and/or demands, subjected to blame when things go wrong, and so on.

What is lack of exposure? It is the inability to see how an unfamiliar or uncomfortable situation is a learning opportunity. How can the unfamiliar and/or discomfort situation be used as a learning opportunity? One can learn and use intentional action steps, including repetition or visualizing, auditory cues, dialogue, intercultural development opportunities, education, reading, attending diverse events, and so on. Exposure consists of personal responsibility, willingness to change, and/or awareness of cultural differences. For instance, all of us have the capacity to learn multiple languages in our lifetime, but the lack of exposure (through education/learning) to those languages impedes us from achieving higher levels of language proficiency.

As mentioned earlier, I realized that I am invisible to some people, even when people interact directly with me. I can sense a level of discomfort on their part. This awareness is not recent; it started when I was a child attending school in Caracas, Venezuela. I was one of the few children with a dark complexion and kinky hair in the school. These attributes made me a target of indifference by a lot of teachers and school personnel. Not until 3rd grade did I experience a sense of belonging. I finally felt that someone, my 3rd-grade teacher, could see me and liked me the way I was.

There have been many studies conducted on racism and discrimination, including about different types of implicit and explicit biases and actions that impact student success. For instance, in 1973, Mary Rowe coined the term "microinequities" to identify the quiet, systematic, sometimes hostile, but often unintentional discrimination of being overlooked, ignored, excluded, or "dissed" (Rowe, 1990). The accumulation of microinequities or microaggressions might seem insignificant to the dominant culture, but they add up to a weight that can feel like hostility.

According to the research, students who are discriminated against because of their ethnicity, race, religion, disability, and so on are more likely to be low performers, miss more school, have less motivation for learning and academic achievement, and higher rates of dropping out of formal education. Ho and Cherng (2018) found parallels in Cherng's childhood experience of being ignored by his teachers while exploring an underresearched topic in parent-involvement literature: the role that students' race and country of birth play in a teacher's likelihood of contacting their parents or guardians to share good or bad news. Ho and Cherng found that the discomfort of the teachers' dealing with diverse families was a crucial and determining factor in terms of whether a parent or guardian would be contacted by the teacher or not (Ho & Cherng, 2018).

In a school context, it is folly to believe that everyone is going to agree on everything, no matter how wonderful the leadership may be. However, seeking shared values and shared goals is an on-going process that may allow the school to be more effective and responsive to its students and families.

ADDITIONAL CONCERNS ABOUT TRUST IN SCHOOLS

The elephant in the room, of course, is that there are some rough things that happen in many schools. Kids do act out, especially when their needs are not being met either at home or at school. This is due, in part, to understaffed, underresourced schools. There are students who can become violent, become bullies, even bullying the teachers, and the teachers cannot help them regulate their behavior. Maybe the school mishandles the situation or doesn't have the resources necessary, doesn't have an emotional-behavioral disorder (EBD) specialist, for example, doesn't have extra space, doesn't have anyone who can deal appropriately with the child or children in question. This is a reality in many schools with no clear answer.

Due to the various cultural conflicts in schools and the inability of schools and other public institutions to defend themselves, there has been a movement not only toward segregated schools but toward privatization and backlash against all things public, including public schools. This movement is larger than only schools and education; there is a strong push to increase privatization, neoliberalism, and backlash against all things public (public schools, public health care, public spaces, disapproval of government). This has had a detrimental effect on these public institutions (Lipman, 2011; Miner, 2013).

So, while public schools are feeling the effects of these attacks, we are reminded of the wise words of educational scholar Pedro Noguera (2003):

> Those who castigate and disparage urban public schools without offering viable solutions for improving or replacing them jeopardize the interests of those who depend on them. . . . Public schools in the United States are the only social institutions that cannot by law turn a child away regardless of race, religion, immigration status, or any other trait or designation (Kirp, 1982) . . . it is also the only public service that functions as a form of social entitlement: a

> "positive right" and social good provided to citizens and noncitizens alike (Carnoy & Levin, 1985). (pp. 6–7)

In response to such claims, a parent might wonder: "What's wrong with parents caring above all for their own child and not all other children, even if this means abandoning public schools? Shouldn't our own children be our number one priority?" In response, we would answer that there is an element of good sense here in that, yes, we must take responsibility for our own children first. That is entirely understandable. And many parents struggle to accomplish this. However, looking more broadly, we must ask, is a world in which parents are only concerned about their own children the world we want for our children? What are the effects of large numbers of parents placing their entire concern with their own children while neglecting concern for the education of all children?

To better answer the question, "What is wrong with parents only caring about their own child?" Our answer is that this approach does not lead to inclusive and responsive schools, and does not prioritize the teaching of socialization into a multicultural society or of citizenship in a multicultural democracy. A strong priority on one's own child at the expense of public schools or the common good makes communal projects, like public schools, more difficult, and especially for poor and working-class children. The privatization of schools treats schools as commodities, not as inclusive and responsive localized communities, and public schools often become underfunded and even more segregated as a result (Miner, 2013).

What if we flipped the script? There is a better way. What if we assumed that parents were not just consumers of schools? Schools are not like Burger King, for example, whose tagline is "have it your way." Following Gutmann's *Democratic Education*, schools should be the building blocks of democracy. Schools prepare students for democratic citizenship, and they are also governed collectively. There can and will be controversies. We can't all see everything eye to eye; that is to be expected. But the compromises that need to be made are arguably good for a more cohesive society, through the goal of people learning the needs of others.

Still, we want to consider the question parents may be wondering: "Are there legitimate fears I should have about public schools? And if so, what might they be?" Some parental fear might be legitimate. For example, there may be legitimate concerns about bullying and safety, low-quality instruction, or lack of resources, even though such concerns may also at times be exaggerated on social media, news reports, and in word-of-mouth retellings. Parents should not believe everything they hear about schools based on hearsay, sensationalism in the media for clicks (news media tend to sensationalize news for attention and to grow their audience), or potentially racist and classist fears, which have contributed to school segregation.

We certainly care a great deal about the physical and emotional safety of all students. This must be paramount. However, we know that sometimes healthy challenges (such as culture clashes/priorities) are misinterpreted and exaggerated. We return to this topic in the next chapter.

CONCLUSION

Dr. Martin Luther King Jr. once said, "A genuine leader is not a searcher of consensus but a molder of consensus." This is an important quote to wrestle with because, on the one hand, we want breathing space to be who we want to be and to honor our distinct cultural heritages. On the other hand, in a collective effort, it helps to be rowing in the same direction. Although public schools cannot be all things to all people, they can continuously work to meet the needs of a diverse community. There is no doubt that schools can become more inclusive and responsive institutions, but they are already valuable resources and foundational pillars in our communities. We know the work of integrating a diverse school community is challenging in many ways, but this is good, important work. If schools are successful at doing this important work, our larger diverse communities are more likely capable of working toward shared governance and collaborative problem solving on terms of equality.

In the next chapter, we turn to how parents and educators might work together to improve the conditions of schools. We understand there are different levels of involvement parents may be willing to take to improve not only the education of their own child but perhaps the school their child attends, and even perhaps the larger set of schools in their community and the various social and economic factors that may affect children and families.

DISCUSSION QUESTIONS

1. What did you think about the topics in this chapter? Have you witnessed any of the phenomena that were described here?
2. What do you think are the key misunderstandings among parents and teachers in schools? Are there examples of mixed messages you might have noticed coming from schools?
3. For teachers: How do you handle or think about homework?
4. For parents: What do you think the kind of homework a teacher gives tells you about the curriculum, if anything?
5. For parents: How much do you think is the "right" amount of homework for your child? If the teacher does not assign enough homework to challenge your child, do you know of resources that you could turn to for additional work?
6. Parents (and teachers) are often heard criticizing how schools handle discipline. The school cannot mirror every family's disciplinary style, since they are often in contradiction with one another. Talk about the approach to discipline in the school. Does it represent a particular style? How is discipline handled? Are there ways it could be improved or better understood?
7. If parents of dominant racial, class, and linguistic groups have a louder voice in schools, as research suggests, in what ways might that be a problem?
8. What additional approaches not mentioned in the chapter might help to facilitate greater trust among parents, educators, and students?

CHAPTER 6

Enhanced Parental Involvement in Schools

> Democracy is not a state. It is an act, and each generation must do its part to help build what we called the Beloved Community, a nation and world society at peace with itself. . . . Ordinary people with extraordinary vision can redeem the soul of America by getting in what I call good trouble, necessary trouble.
>
> —John Lewis (2020)

In the previous chapter, we described and encouraged discussion about some of the most challenging aspects of building trust between parents and schools. We also raised the question of whether parents and others may need to advocate for better schools in their communities. The schools our children attend may need additional resources, for example, such as more staff members or repairs or expansion of the school building. Needed changes are often not forthcoming without advocacy and mobilization. In this chapter, we delve deeper into these questions and suggest ways in which parents can become involved and active in supporting their child's education, as well as supporting the larger community's educational offerings.

In part due to inequalities, parents find themselves in many various circumstances, in terms of time, flexibility, and resources. We know a substantial number of parents feel overwhelmed with parenting and the stresses of life in an unequal society. There are also parents who have time and energy to become more involved with supporting their child's school or the community's larger school system on a volunteer basis. In this chapter, we suggest ways parents might be productively involved with their children's education and school at various levels of engagement.

IT MAY TAKE A VILLAGE, BUT PARENTS' FIRST PRIORITY IS THEIR OWN FAMILY

As we argued in the introduction, parents are children's first and most influential teachers. It is hard to overstate the importance of parents in the education and development of their children. Of course, different families have different parenting styles and unique circumstances. We do not suggest there is one best way to parent a child, but we encourage all parents to continue learning and searching for resources and information to support their children.

The first and arguably most important task in parenting is to love and encourage our children. This includes providing a safe and healthy environment for them as much as possible. We realize this is not an easy task, given financial and other pressures. Parents also provide intellectual and physical stimulation. Children learn their native language from their parents, although they may soon need to learn a second or third language as they grow and become socialized beyond the family, or even within a multilingual family. Parents offer supportive conversations, family activities, cooking and eating healthy food together, playing, taking part in informal or formal athletics, visiting family, and so on. We suggest reading together with children as much as possible, which research has found has many emotional and academic benefits (Knoester, 2009; 2010; Knoester & Plikuhn, 2015; 2016).

Parents make sure their children attend school on time and every day. They provide social opportunities for their children with other children outside of school. Parents bring their children to the pediatrician on a regular basis and in times of a sickness or injury that may require treatment. Parents provide clothing adequate for the weather and wash it regularly. They also communicate with the school, follow up on paperwork, monitor their children's progress, attend school events, encourage their children to try their best in school, show curiosity about what their children are learning, encourage and model kindness and respect toward others, and teach their children to become more curious, independent, and stronger every day. These are the basics, right? If parents are able to do these things, that is a significant victory. Of course, we know there are obstacles many families face that make achieving these goals difficult, and it is important to give parents the benefit of the doubt and provide support, whenever possible. Many families have larger extended families that can provide crucial support. Schools can also point to resources in the community that may assist with various aspects of parenting and provide information and meeting spaces for parents to learn from one another.

VOLUNTEERING IN THE SCHOOL

Beyond taking care of one's own children and preparing them for success in school and in life, some parents have time and interest for additional ways to support the school. One key way is through volunteering in the school. Eliciting parental collaboration and involvement starts with the school. According to longtime teacher, union president, and school board member Bob Peterson (personal communication, October 23, 2023), schools should, first of all, encourage all members of the school—all families—to feel welcome to participate in the life of the school. There are so many ways parents can volunteer in schools, depending on what the school requests, from assisting teachers in their classrooms to tutoring children during or after school, helping to serve breakfast or lunch, monitoring recess, helping to put together family communications, putting up bulletin boards, chaperoning field trips, and much more.

As Murphy and Torre (2014) suggest,

> To increase involvement within the school, leaders must collaborate with parents to devise coherent ways for parents to volunteer. Collaboration is essential for matching parent assets to the needs of the school. Volunteer opportunities within the school should be managed by school staff and parents to maximize the impact of the parent's time and effort. Ideally, volunteers would help where their particular skills were most beneficial, would have clear guidelines for what they should be doing, and would become an integral part of the classroom. (Haynes & Ben-Avie, 1996) (p. 183)

Volunteering not only allows the school to accomplish tasks that might not otherwise be done but also provides additional opportunities for teachers and other staff members to learn more from parents, which could be beneficial in connecting with and better understanding students. Parents can also learn about the thinking of teachers and other school personnel and about the many demands on educators' time.

Reflecting on her extensive teaching career, Lynne Yermanock Streib (2010) wrote about the significant positive role parent volunteers played in the life of her classroom:

> Parent involvement was important to me because of the many contributions parents made. They were additional adults in the classroom. They listened to children, read to them, and helped them with academic work. They allowed us to do intensive hands-on activities like cooking and crafts, which would have been more difficult otherwise. They taught the children and me about themselves and things they knew. They enriched our studies with their knowledge, experiences, and resources. Though I taught for many years and taught many of the same things year after year, it was the children and their parents who made each year different and special. (p. 165)

This passage reminds us that the collaboration between teachers and parents can be many things. Beyond providing information and help to the education of children, these relationships can also be meaningful in and of themselves, forming the building blocks of a nurturing community.

As discussed in the previous chapter, in pursuit of an inclusive school community, we caution parents to be aware of race and class dynamics of entitlement when they become involved in school activities and volunteering. Research and personal experience have shown that White and middle- and upper-class parents are too often given more power in schools, and their voices can drown out parents of color and parents who are less likely to attend parent meetings (Horvat et al., 2003; Posey-Maddox, 2014).

It is fair to assume that all parents care about the education of their children. All parents' voices need to be heard and considered by the school, whether or not those parents attend meetings or volunteer in the school. Aside from attending meetings, voices can be heard and valued through the use of written surveys, phone calls, personal conversations, or other information gathering that best represent all voices and not only the parents who are most active in the school. And schools should be as intentional as possible about increasing participation with strong and clear communication and also by seeking resources, such as bus tickets, other forms of transportation, and providing child care and food at meetings so parent gatherings can be as accessible as possible. Policies and activities in schools must be continually analyzed and reflected on to determine whether they can become more inclusive and responsive to parental concerns.

ADVOCACY AT THE CITY LEVEL

If parents wish to advocate directly to the school board, they will be more effective if they understand the district's procedures and policies when it comes to questioning, sharing concerns, and so on. It is important to learn who to go to within the school district, which is essential to getting things done. It is not advisable to simply publicly attack the district administration. Sometimes, school board members do need to be pushed and pressured. However, smaller problems can usually be dealt with most effectively at the school level. Simple questions are important to ask—is there a PTA? (Parent Teacher Association, chapter of a national organization) or a PTO (parent–teacher organization that is not tied to a national organization)? What can take place within the existing organizational structures? Is there a council at the school that helps guide the staff? What can be done within these bodies?

These are questions that cannot be given a single broad answer, as they depend on the specific needs and histories of individual schools and communities.

Other reminders about school-level involvement we would like to offer are:

- Try to be helpful without crowding out other voices.
- Build partnerships between parents and educators to create two-way forms of communication.
- Support spaces where parents can meet and learn from one another.

- Remember that most parents are trying their best to help their children succeed in school.
- Recognize that parenting, teaching, and administration of schools are hard jobs, and everyone should be given grace and the benefit of the doubt.
- Whenever it is overheard, interrupt the shaming or blaming of poor/struggling families, single-parent families, parents who are quiet/overwhelmed/intimidated to show up at school events. Remember that many parents are also likely hiding personal struggles (we know this from research and personal experiences). Build solidarity.

Schools are intimately connected with their surrounding communities. There are many ways for parents to support and advocate for their child's school or the larger city's schools. Many of the challenges we see in schools are the result of out-of-school factors, including poverty, lack of quality transportation, housing, food, jobs, and health care, including mental health care. These are all areas that require action from an organized community to improve the quality of life for families.

As Jean Anyon (2014) reminds us:

> Low-achieving urban schools are not primarily a consequence of failed education policy, urban family dynamics, underprepared teachers, or too few tests—as mainstream analysts and public policies typically imply. Failing public schools in cities are, rather, a logical consequence of the U.S. political economy—and the federal and regional policies and practices that support it. Teachers, principals, and the urban students are not the culprits—as reform policies that target high stakes testing, educator quality, and the control of youth assume. Rather, an unjust economy and the policies through which it is maintained create barriers to educational success that no teacher or principal practice, no standardized test, and no "zero tolerance" policy can surmount for long. It is for this reason that I argue that *macroeconomic mandates continually trump urban educational policy and school reform.* (pp. 4–5, italics in the original)

We agree with Anyon that educational outcomes (such as standardized test scores, graduate rates, college entrance rates, etc.)

are intricately connected to quality-of-life factors that are generally not understood to be education-related. Imagine if a child has a toothache and is not able to see a dentist: This child's academic progress may be halted because they do not have access to a dentist and the pain is distracting from schoolwork. Imagine if a child spends most of their time being transported from one place to another: This is a transportation issue that can also cause stress and distraction if the mode of transit is not reliable. Imagine if a child does not receive enough nutrition: This is a policy issue, since schools can provide better food, and some families live many miles away from a grocery store or face other barriers, all of which can affect the child's ability to learn. Imagine if a child has experienced trauma and does not receive therapy or a safer environment: These are issues that can at least partially be addressed with better policy. As Darling-Hammond (2010; Knoester, 2013) argued and showed with evidence, targeted policies can and have addressed each of these issues. Lyndon Johnson's "War on Poverty" had a significant positive effect on closing the "achievement gap" in U.S. schools, but neoliberal policies of the 1980s rolled back these gains. They were necessary then and they are necessary now.

ORGANIZING IN BUFFALO, NEW YORK

Allow me (Hervé) to share a personal example of community organizing in my community. In 2006, when I was in graduate school and my two oldest children were in elementary school, a group of African parents in Buffalo, New York, where I was then living, became disappointed at the rate of disaffection of their children and other minority children in the educational system in Buffalo. We decided that we needed to do something. The platform we created was called the African Education Alliance Taskforce. It was headed by Dr. Haoua Hamza, who served as chair, Mulu Belete as vice chair, and I served as secretary of the group, alongside committed parents and community members, including teachers, priests, and pastors.

We started advocating for African refugee students, who we perceived needed specific attention, as they were going through unique challenges. Many of these immigrant students were challenged by interrupted formal education due to the strife in their home countries, living in refugee camps, and eventually moving to the United States. Due to wars taking place in their homelands, several students never had the chance to attend formal schools at all. To quote an African proverb, "If the antelope is erring, it is because its abode is awash with water." Among the African refugee students, several had been forced to serve as child soldiers and to witness, or even be involved with, what we would consider atrocities, before they were able to escape. To use figurative language, they came to the American school with their two hands loaded with heavy suitcases full of stones, with which they were expected to climb the educational ladder as if they were "normal" children who had a chance to experience a carefree childhood.

Our activities and initiatives as part of the African Education Alliance Taskforce included meeting with heads of community agencies and organizations interested in reaching out and working with the African immigrant and refugee community on issues such as employment, housing, health care (including mental health), and education. We also held an African night, which was a cultural and scholarship dinner. As Zehr (2001) reminds us, the description of many African newcomers captures why many of these students struggle in school:

> Some of them have witnessed fighting firsthand and lost close family members to the ravages of war, others were forced to flee their homeland and live in crowded refugee camps . . . or on the fringes of African cities, often for years . . . education is pretty limited and for cultural reasons, girls attend schools less than boys . . . some children don't go to school because they are hungry; they suffer hunger-induced headaches and find it hard to concentrate on class work . . . many never became literate in their own tongue . . . [they] have academic as well as language barriers . . . they come here—and it may be the first time they think of school as a building. They've never stood in a lunch line. They have never had to return a library book. (pp. 1–2)

Teachers in the United States may not be cognizant of the obstacles to learning that their students face. If basic human needs are not met, it is difficult to expect the higher needs on Maslow's pyramid of needs to be satisfied.

The onus is perhaps on the parents to educate their children's teacher about their current situation in order to ease the channels of communication. However, many parents are not able to do so. Perhaps it should go without saying that a one-size-fits-all approach to all students will not adequately address the educational lag of the students just described. These students had been transplanted into totally new geographical and cultural places, but they also came with a cultural capital that had little currency in American schools.

Our group started raising awareness about these special segments of our student population. Without ascribing to ourselves any messianic vantage point, although not oblivious to our own social positions as relatively privileged, we started by creating a cadre where parents could meet and foster a community of people of goodwill who could empower themselves to speak up for their children. Figuratively speaking, we were of the mind that 1,000 chickens organized and committed could drive away a preying hawk (in a more literal sense, to drive away the fear and inhibitions that prevent otherwise powerless people from speaking up for themselves and for their children). Schools have policies, but they are not necessarily enforced unless parents and members of the community hold schools to them. For example, the No Child Left Behind Act, despite being a far from perfect piece of legislation, delineated rights and goals for parents of English language learners. This language could be pointed to and compared to what we were seeing in schools. The legislation sought to require that:

1. All students must be taught by a highly qualified teacher.
2. Children must be taught using research-based best practices.
3. Children must have the opportunity to reach their greatest academic potential.

All of these goals and principles looked great on paper. However, it requires parents and community members to work with schools as partners and witnesses to ensure that they come true.

We met with the curriculum director of the Buffalo Public Schools, and finally, we had several working sessions with the superintendent and his staff to apprise them of the plight of the immigrant children as we understood it. We organized workshops for parents and teachers to raise their awareness and share ideas about how to best assist immigrant students toward their academic success. As the Syracuse School Board heard about the good job we were doing in Buffalo, they invited us to hold a workshop with their teachers as well. Many of the teachers we worked with confessed to us that with the increasing numbers of immigrant students in their schools, they did not think they were meeting the needs of those students, although they struggled to identify what course of action they should take. The most intractable hurdle seemed to be intercultural communication. The teachers meant well, but they felt clueless as to how to best meet the needs of these students. Again, one can barely teach what one does not know (Howard, 2016).

As alluded to, we institutionalized an African Student Night and raised money for scholarships based on need. During the African Student Night, we also gave students awards based on academic merit, participation in after-school activities such as dance and sports, and enjoyed an evening of sharing food and conversation in a true collectivist African spirit. These kinds of gatherings, we believe, encouraged a sense of pride in their culture and reminded students that they were surrounded by adults who cared about their success.

We found that when parents and community members are involved in the lives of students, teachers and schools become more responsive to the needs of their students, especially those who may be vulnerable for failure.

These activities are consistent with the belief that learning cannot be understood purely in cognitive or academic terms. Learning is also relational (and economic and social). Unfortunately, schools have often placed too much emphasis on thinking processes. In their defense, schools are not always free to choose whatever course they deem best for the local community, as they are often subjugated to macro policies that give them little leeway. This is not to say that we should repudiate cognitive processes in schools, but students are human beings, made of flesh and blood, gray matter, nerves, and much more. Students bring their "whole selves" and should be recognized and accepted as such.

As noted previously, the demographics in our schools are shifting, not unlike the rest of society. Students bring to school their whole selves and schools generally cannot choose which type of students to enroll. Therefore, schools must be places where students of all types want to go and learn. We can do a better job of developing curricula that build on the interests and experiences of the students who enroll, encouraging all students to aspire to their greatest selves.

ORGANIZING IN SOUTHERN INDIANA

Permit me (Maura) to share another example of community organizing in support of schools. I started my company, Inclusion and Beyond, Inc., at the beginning of what has been called the "Latino Explosion" in Indiana in 1994. Even though Latinos have been present in Indiana for many generations, a large influx of Latinos at the same time was extremely impactful and rare. In the past, migrants tended to move to urban areas only. This migration had a great effect in the rural areas as well. I also observed that this migration pattern was impacting rural areas not only in southern Indiana but around the country, and not only an influx of Latinos but migrants from many other countries as well.

Since that time, I have worked with various school corporations (districts) in southern Indiana, helping schools get to know these new migrant families, which took a lot of work. The following barriers were some of the issues that affected communication with schools: the language barrier, parents' literacy levels (many of the families didn't know how to read and write in their native language or in English), and building trust and the understanding of families about why school and socialization were some of the key elements to prepare children for their future and to enter the workforce. These continue to be the main barriers that migrant families and schools face.

In 2010, I was hired by Vanderburgh County School District in southern Indiana to provide professional development sessions focusing on family engagement principles for teachers of 35 schools in the district, along with 35 diverse families. We met four times during the school year 2010–2011 for 6 hours each time. I introduced a framework I created for student success and family engagement that I called "Connecting the Dots." Drawing on research, personal experiences, group exercises, and case studies, I had participants discuss and share reflective and newly learned knowledge. Some of the teachers already knew some of the families. My first group exercise created "the magic" for the rest of the six sessions. I created a group exercise as an icebreaker, and each participant had to learn as much as they could from each other during the exercise. The exercise was supposed to last 45 minutes and ended up lasting 4 hours, and several of the teachers came to me after 30 minutes and asked to extend the exercise. One teacher said to me that even though he had spoken to this particular parent during parent–teacher conferences, he felt that this exercise helped him see the parent in a different light. The other teachers chimed in and said the same thing.

Three-fourths of the parents attending this professional training were people of color, while three-fourths of the teachers were White. Understanding, communicating, dealing, and engaging with families takes time and direct contact with others. I noticed that a lack of time to engage with families is a huge concern for teachers. This experience demonstrated that creating a forum for teachers and families to meet and get to know each other is essential.

In my work, I have found that schools' partnerships with community organizations are essential. At another point I was working with rural schools in Daviess County, Indiana. Teachers there were looking for funding to assist some of the students who needed clothing, food, and mental health assistance. They didn't know what to do. The schools didn't have the budget to cover these needs. So, I went into the community to search for resources and found five organizations that were able to provide all the resources needed. I also discovered that these organizations had been trying to get to the schools, but every time they tried, they were turned down. I went back to the schools, and none of them were aware that these organizations were trying to help the students. Within a week, I organized a meeting with all these organizations, the superintendent, and principals. By the end of the meeting, partnerships with all these organizations were created, and as far as I know, they are still working together more than 10 years later.

SUGGESTIONS FOR ORGANIZING

As the examples suggest, different communities need different things. Parents, teachers, and community members and organizations who can put in substantial time and effort into organizing, not only for better schools but for better living conditions, undoubtedly can positively affect student learning. Anyon (2014), building on the work of Chicago-based Cross City Campaign for Urban School Reform (Cahill, 1999) and the Institute for Education and Social Policy in New York (Zimmer & Mediratta, 2004), makes the following recommendations for grassroots community organizing:

1. Choose issues from the bottom up. Issues to pursue should come from parents, students, and other residents. Knock on doors in two-people teams (for example, one parent and one teacher or principal) to identify issues important to the community; and recruit people for home meetings to discuss the issues they feel are important and what to do about them. Visit area congregations to discuss local problems and develop relationships with members and clergy. Systematic personal contact and the building of personal relationships are key to successful engagement of residents.
2. Begin to build a community constituency for long-range reform through immediate, specific, and winnable issues. Frame broad demands like "better schools" more specifically to attract particular constituencies: bilingual programs for Latino parents; after-school job training and placement for parents and high school students. Building a base among parents and community members will provide a force and legitimacy to the demands you will make. Because you also want to develop working relationships with other educators, it may be best to start with a neighborhood issue like jobs and housing rather than one that directly targets problems in the school.
3. Locate key school and district personnel who can assist you in gathering data to document the problems you want to address. Work with local community-based

organizations to see what system information they already have. Collaborate with them, if possible.

4. Develop a program of needed changes and present this to authorities. Plan demonstrations and other activities that attempt to obtain concessions, promises, and behavioral responses from those in power in the district and city.
5. Develop a plan for what to do when people in power ignore you, refer you to others, delay you, try to pacify and placate you, or try to divide and conquer your group. Officials may try to discredit you or pursue action against you. Or they may attempt to buy off your leaders or propose a substitute that does not meet your needs. Some of the strategies you could consider when this happens may be cooperative, like setting up meetings; but some may be confrontational—like pickets, demonstrations, political theatre, press conferences, etc.
6. Keep the pressure on administrators and officials by demonstrations and actions of various sorts. A "presence in the streets" is necessary to hold their attention and get results. (pp. 182–183)

Gorski (2018) summarized a set of initiatives that might make a significant difference for families and schools today in a variety of educational settings:

> Initiative One: Advocate for Universal Preschool and Kindergarten; Initiative Two: Advocate for Smaller Class Sizes; Initiative Three: Extend Health Services and Screenings at Schools; Initiative Four: Protect Physical Education and Recess and Encourage Fitness; Initiative Five: Protect Arts Programs; Initiative Six: Protect School and Local Libraries in High-Poverty Neighborhoods; Initiative Seven: Resist Neoliberal School Reform Initiatives. (pp. 178–182)

The challenges of schools are connected with larger community needs. Gorski describes another set of initiatives that he describes as "policy advocacy for societal justice":

> Initiative One: Advocate for Living-Wage Laws; Initiative Two: Advocate for Affordable Housing Policies and Tenant Rights;

> Initiative Three: Advocate for Universal Health Care; Initiative Four: Advocate for Environmental Justice. (pp. 183–184)

These recommendations make clear that school reform and structural reform in neighborhoods are intimately related, and building coalitions might include groups that work on various separate but interrelated issues. Each of these lists of initiatives would affect not only the quality of life of children and families but also the quality of education that students receive.

CONCLUSION

This chapter has focused on various ways parents might be involved in their own child's education, in their child's school, and in the larger community. Some families have more time, energy, and interest in being involved in their child's education and school than others. Of course, the most basic tasks of parenting are to love our children and to provide a safe and healthy environment for them. Parents provide healthy food, a quiet place to sleep and rest, and ideally a safe place to play. They bring children to their pediatrician regularly. Parents of school-age children make sure they get to school on time and try to get them to read on a regular basis and to do their homework. They also give children social opportunities and stimulation, such as bringing them to visit family and other outings. Those are some of the basic tasks, not a complete list. However, some parents struggle significantly with items on this list.

We ask a lot of parents in this country with fewer safeguards or social safety nets as compared to other industrialized nations. For example, most states in the United States do not require employers to provide paid family leave, health insurance for part-time workers, or even to provide a living wage. Many locations do not have adequate, fast, and reliable public transportation, or affordable housing. These are issues that may require concerted effort to pass policies that can help to make raising a family more feasible. We also know that some families may not be aware of the community resources that are available to them. It may be helpful to know that schools often employ social workers who can help connect parents to local resources, such as shelters, food, dental clinics, and transportation.

Taking care of one's children is the first task of parenting, but some parents have additional time, energy, and interest in becoming more involved with supporting the school and larger community. They want to see their child's school thrive. There are many volunteer opportunities that may be available. Examples might include working in classrooms, especially with younger children; leading a small group of students; helping the teacher organize the classroom or to file papers. It depends in part on a parent's particular interests and skill set. It is also important that parents from dominant cultures not drown out other voices. Such a dynamic can send an unwelcoming message and create the perception that only some voices matter, such as college-educated parents, for example, or that these parents should have more say in what should be the priorities of the school.

In summary, we discussed at length ways in which parents, teachers, and other community members who have the passion and interest in improving schools can become more involved in their communities. There are many community issues that may not be normally understood to be connected with schooling. However, when we consider some of the real struggles children and families face, there are policy initiatives that can address these challenges that might be enacted with enough political pressure from the community.

The ways in which parents feel they can be involved in their child's education and in the community are ultimately decisions that are made at the personal level. We wrote this chapter not to recommend specific actions but with the hope that parents and teachers can recognize and respect how interconnected these issues are and to work however possible to make improvements in their communities and in their children's educations.

DISCUSSION QUESTIONS

1. How would you summarize this chapter?
2. What are the primary concerns raised in this chapter?
3. Does it matter whether some parent voices are stronger than others within a school? If so, in what ways?

4. What are steps schools could take to ensure all parent voices and concerns are being heard and addressed?
5. If you could get the school board or superintendent to make one change, what would it be?
6. How might parents and educators continue to build community partnerships to better support students' success and needs?

CHAPTER 7

Conclusion

> Multicultural citizenship is essential for today's global age. . . . It recognizes and legitimizes the rights and needs of citizens to maintain commitments both to their cultural communities and to the national civic culture.
>
> —James A. Banks (2007)

In this final chapter, we return to the central themes of the book. Schooling is part of a socialization process within a multicultural society. Students do not attend school simply to become employable, although that is part of it. Education is cultural work that intentionally prepares students to become knowledgeable and thoughtful citizens in a democracy. The deeper goal is to learn to live in a democratic, multicultural society, working across cultural divides to solve problems. Segregation, inequality, and political divisions in the larger society, as well as within schools themselves, have made this goal more challenging but even more important.

We do not take the promise of democracy in the United States for granted or view these issues as idle wishes. These issues are existential, important not only for individuals and communities but for the survival of multicultural democracy itself and for the rights and privileges it enables. Two of us are immigrants from countries (Venezuela and Burkina Faso) that have struggled—and have largely failed, especially in recent years—to secure democratic rights and freedoms for their people. We are Americans, all three of us, and care deeply about democratic values in the United States, but nevertheless believe the government and its schools can become more inclusive and responsive to its people, to become "a more perfect union," in the words of the U.S. Constitution. We have also seen democratic norms, values, and laws slip away in countries that we love, and we do not want to see that happen in the United States. We challenge readers to continually ask, what is necessary to become a more egalitarian, effective, and intentional democratic citizen? How can we learn to counter negative stereotypes perpetuated about various cultural groups, who are then used by opportunistic politicians as scapegoats as they pit various groups against one another? How can we teach our children to be curious about and to respect cultural differences, to become empathetic to the struggles of others and better able to work together to solve shared goals?

We have offered a number of ideas in this book about how to do so and have encouraged discussion about what these issues may look like in your community. We can also look outside of our country's borders for ideas about how to improve our schools. Finland, for example, is a country that has gained an international reputation for impressive educational progress, based on a large variety of measures, including high graduation rates, equity across economic groups, and high average scores on international tests (Sahlberg, 2021). Finnish universities are highly selective for their teacher education programs, but they are free of charge. Once hired, teachers spend a significant portion of every day preparing for their next lesson and reflecting on past lessons and either mentoring or being mentored by colleagues (as opposed to the United States, where teachers are in front of students for almost the entire day). Finland provides professional development that is powerful throughout teachers' careers and offers adult education throughout the lifespan. Teachers' pay and benefits are higher as compared to teachers in the United States. Education is celebrated in Finnish culture, and teachers are respected and their opinions heard in public discourse. Finland also has a powerful and effective social safety net: Food, housing, and health care are free or highly accessible, so economic inequality is much lower, which has positive effects on school outcomes (Sahlberg, 2021). There are many other differences between the United States and Finland that make easy comparisons difficult, but this example suggests that the educational struggles we experience in the United States are not inevitable and that it is possible to imagine a society organized to be more supportive of families and schools (Knoester, 2013).

Darling-Hammond (2010) notes that one of the greatest challenges in U.S. education is addressing the achievement gap between White and Asian American students on the one hand and Black and Latino/a children on the other. This gap threatens the future success of U.S. education, given demographic changes. It is crucial for the health of democracy and for economic growth that schools treat students of color with greater respect and investment. This includes addressing school segregation and the disparities in funding between schools serving different socioeconomic groups.

The ways we currently evaluate schools must be rethought. Standardized tests cannot be the sole measure of what constitutes a successful school, or successful students. These tests are inaccurate, and they do not take into account some of the most fundamental goals of education that we've outlined in this book. Schools need better measures of success. Better assessments of schools and students might include a combination of graduation rates, college acceptance rates, attendance rates, referral rates, evaluation of student work such as portfolios, and fundamentally, reserving judgment for the educators and adults who know the students best (Knoester, 2008; Knoester & Au, 2017; Meier & Knoester, 2017).

EDUCATION AND DEMOCRACY

In a multicultural democracy, schools should center education on preparation for democratic life. In practicing democracy in schools, we hope to educate skilled and feisty children who can lead in the future, unafraid of and knowledgeable about people culturally different from themselves and prepared to tackle difficult social challenges together. Schools must be about more than ranking, elitism, or limiting education to job attainment. Educators, parents, and community members may face disagreements, impasses, contradictions, and an imperfect process for making decisions. But deliberation and reaching agreements on priorities are the good work of schools. We hope this book has offered an opportunity for reflection and discussion about how to make schools more inclusive and responsive for everyone involved.

In this book, we have asked readers to think about and discuss what is needed for educators and parents to build trust across cultural differences. What are the elements needed to make it work? If we cannot figure out these questions in schools, it is many times more difficult to figure them out for the larger society. Without trust, our democratic institutions break down, eventually leading to top-down authoritarianism and the elimination of individual civil rights and investments in education. We should seriously think about the implications of failure.

At the risk of putting too fine a point on it, U.S. democracy may be facing an existential crisis of its own. As seen in countries with which the authors are very familiar (our native countries), the United States could become ungovernable if democratic norms are not upheld. As we saw in the middle of the 20th century, fascism (and the pseudo-fascism we have seen in parts of the United States) depends on scapegoating the "other." In the United States, the suffering of ordinary working people is blamed by demagogues on "them": people of color, immigrants, LGBTQ+, and others, rather than on the wealthy, who have the power to change the economic structure (Knoester & Knoester, 2023). Scapegoating the most marginalized groups leads to increased suffering, mistrust, and a breakdown of norms needed for a functional democratic society.

These kinds of arguments about governance, democracy, and sociology are challenging for many people to comprehend, in part because these ideas are abstract and people are separated from and often unable to understand and care about the circumstances of others. Without direct knowledge of people culturally different from oneself, it is difficult to notice and to counter the scapegoating that is taking place. Ordinary people are understandably focused on their immediate needs, and individualism is highly prized in the United States (Foner, 1998).

It may be useful to reframe abstract concepts such as "democracy" and "democratic norms" into more concrete concepts, such as civil rights, the right to vote, the right to free speech, the right to practice one's religion, and the right to a public education. These are material rights, inscribed into law, and are important because democracy depends on them (unlike in monarchies or dictatorships). But we know democracy—including all of the civil rights that accompany it—can be lost. Americans tend to view the loss of civil rights as only a distant possibility. However, those of us from countries like Burkina Faso and Venezuela know this feeling well. We feel it deeply and know the erosion of civil rights can happen swiftly.

Civil rights, such as the right to vote and the right to speak freely against the government without being imprisoned, need to be defended and strengthened and understood by ordinary citizens. The danger of losing rights is hard to see in a place like the United States. Like a fish's knowledge of water, to use the common metaphor, it is hard to be self-reflective of one's own circumstances without seeing it from an outsider's perspective.

For example, before the reign of Hugo Chávez and now Nicolás Maduro, Venezuela was one of the most democratic and economically thriving countries in Central and South America. The implementation of authoritarian rule nearly 3 decades ago—which undermined free and fair elections, and imprisoned political opponents, among many other violations of democratic norms—has led to approximately 7 million Venezuelans fleeing the country in search of a better life for themselves and their children (Muñoz-Pogossian & Winkler, 2023). Inflation and the poverty rate skyrocketed. This situation is not entirely removed from the United States, or from U.S. schools, considering there are approximately 1 million migrants and refugees in the United States from Venezuela, about one in five of whom is a child of school age (Freedom House, 2023).

Turning to the case of Burkina Faso, a similar story has unfolded. We can notice how the use of rhetoric such as "patriotism" has been used to hide deeply undemocratic maneuvers. Burkina Faso, like Venezuela, was once hailed for its strong culture of democracy. However, in recent decades the country was thrown into a maelstrom of seemingly unending military takeovers, each followed by glimmers of hope with the appearance of a democratic election, only to be overthrown once again by the military. Poverty, illiteracy rates, and continued violence have accompanied these events (Freedom House, 2024).

In both Venezuela and Burkina Faso, we notice that when democracy is overthrown, civil rights can disappear quickly. Social spending and investments in people, such as education and health care, diminish. People in the United States do not seem to realize that their civil rights and the right to an education are unique to a democracy, and these rights need to be defended. After all, why would a dictator seek to invest in the education of its citizens when the dictator seeks control over all decisions?

As we have tried to make clear throughout this book, education within a multicultural but segregated country plays a pivotal role in supporting democracy. Within a multicultural school, educators, students, and parents must work together to overcome negative stereotypes; learn to understand and appreciate one another's viewpoints and experiences; and build trusting relationships in order to work together to address shared challenges in a multicultural democratic society, even if it is difficult.

SUMMARY OF THE BOOK

This book was written to address what we perceive to be a lack of books and resources written for parents of school-age children and for educators, with a particular focus on fostering dialogue and special attention to multicultural education. Using personal stories from the three authors—as well as drawing on empirical and theoretical research, and providing discussion questions at the end of each chapter—we have argued that among the many purposes of schools, education for democratic citizenship in a multicultural society should be a top priority. This book has described both struggles and successful family–school collaborations, powerful culturally relevant educational experiences, and effective communication models. It has also offered strategies parents and educators can use to improve communication, partnerships, cultural awareness, and to become stronger advocates for public schools in their communities.

Drawing on empirical research, the book has described larger patterns of inequalities and has suggested ways in which families and schools can work together to optimize the academic, social, and emotional development of all students, with particular focus on students experiencing poverty, immigrants, and students of color. The book has been critical of the prevailing deficit view of families and children and offered information and suggestions for ways all parents and children to be better heard and understood (González et al., 2005). Each chapter elicits discussion so parents can better understand the work of schools more generally and educators can learn from families. Through all of these methods, the book provides tools and encouragement to help parents and educators with different values and viewpoints better communicate, understand, and collaborate for the benefit of all children.

We have included reflections on our work as educators, parents, scholars, and activists for inclusive education. We hope these stories and suggestions serve as a resource for more thoughtful, intentional parenting of school-age children and for family–school partnerships that focus not only on the success of one's own child but also toward a more community-oriented viewpoint, mindful of all of the children and adults involved in education.

In the first chapter, we discussed education as a cultural intervention (Knoester & Yu, 2015). Parents may wonder why a particular subject they would like their child to learn is not taught in school. Why does the school teach x but not y? Subjects not taught in school might be highly beneficial for students to learn and may have powerful real-world applications. This is a frequent concern and topic of discussion in many school communities. Schools and districts must make difficult choices because, due to limited time and resources (especially teacher qualifications), schools cannot be all things to all people.

In considering the educational needs of a democracy, it is important to ask what kinds of knowledge and dispositions are necessary to become active and effective citizens (Gutmann, 1999). Unfortunately, evidence suggests that the educational preparation of current citizens leaves much to be desired (Knoester & Gichiru, 2021). Further, scarcity of time and resources creates conflict because parents may assume that the school's role is to enhance their family's culture and priorities. In terms of setting priorities, there needs to be some moderation, flexibility, and understanding on all sides (Kliebard, 2004). However, multicultural education (Banks, 2015) and culturally relevant pedagogy (Ladson-Billings, 2014) must be central aspects of an education that seeks inclusion and responsive preparation for citizenship and academic success.

In Chapter 2, we made the case that diverse and integrated schools have many benefits that are undervalued. We argued that racially integrated schools create heightened conditions for learning intercultural competence and summarized research literature finding many beneficial outcomes of integrated schools. We also noted that the way *Brown v. Board of Education* was carried out had many flaws and placed Black students, families, and communities in horrendous situations in many locations. The integration of schools on terms of equality is ongoing work that requires thoughtful and intentional work to interrupt and end forces of White supremacy and to create optimal conditions for developing intercultural competence.

In Chapter 3, we extended our argument that schooling is a socialization process, worthy of reflection and investment by all involved. Socialization is not only about children making new friends at school, although that is important. Schools are also places where children (and adults) learn to respect, appreciate, and come to understand the knowledge and struggles of people who may be culturally different and have different experiences from themselves. The chapter began with Hervé's experience of being educated in Burkina Faso and then immigrating to the United States as an adult and sending his children to U.S. schools. He stressed how knowledge and appreciation for different cultures, or intercultural competence, can and should become increasingly sophisticated as children grow older, but it is not inevitable. Noticing cultural differences can just as easily lead to disrespect as to appreciation and being viewed as a source of valuable knowledge (Apple, 2014). Intercultural competence requires intentional work and should be part of a curriculum that educates for democratic citizenship.

Chapter 4 focused on how schools and parents can communicate more effectively about the curricular offerings at the school so parents can better support their children's learning. We argued that school systems tend to undervalue two-way communication and rarely have a full-time staff person at each school who is trained in written and oral communication with families and dedicated to that task. Communication about curricula is particularly lacking. With effective communication about ongoing curricula, families can better understand the experiences of their children and support and enhance their child's learning.

Chapter 4 also discussed and problematized the overuse of high-stakes standardized tests. These tests are inaccurate and too often misleading gauges of student learning that incentivize harmful practices (Meier & Knoester, 2017). We argue that there are more effective assessments of student learning that support the central goals of educating for democratic citizenship. We encourage parents to take test scores with a grain of salt and note there are other ways they can monitor their child's progress in school by focusing on children's effort and engagement with school activities, carefully reviewing communications from teachers and the school, and providing outside-of-school reading and other learning opportunities. In this chapter, and the next, we paid particular attention to differentiation and students with Individualized Education Programs (IEPs) or 504 plans. Parent meetings and advocacy are necessary to create effective two-way communication and support for students' individual needs.

In Chapter 5, we focused on some of the most challenging aspects of building trust between families and schools. We discussed topics like discipline and homework and suggested that even great communication may not be enough when schools and parents are fundamentally at odds on priorities. For difficult conversations, carefully planned meetings are beneficial, as well as ongoing discussion. We discussed racial bias, "White fragility," and the social stigma around discussing race, especially in White-dominant communities. We discussed research showing how White and middle-class parents seem to dominate parent groups, including within diverse schools. We also suggested book clubs, such as around the present book, as one example of how to come to deeper understanding of different cultural values around sensitive topics and how all students, parents, and educators can be treated with dignity and respect.

In Chapter 6, we suggested ways in which parents can be involved and active in improving their school's—and the larger community's—educational offerings and resources. Parents are in various circumstances, and many are overwhelmed with parenting and the stresses of life in an unequal society. We suggested a few key ways parents can support their children at home and in school. There are also parents who have time and energy to become more involved with supporting their child's school via volunteering. We caution parents to be aware of race and class dynamics of entitlement. Specifically, research has shown that White and middle- and upper-class parents are too often given more power in schools, and their voices can drown out parents of color and parents who are less likely to attend parent meetings (Horvat et al., 2003; Posey-Maddox, 2014). All parents care about the education of their children, and their voices must be heard and considered, whether or not those parents attend meetings or are otherwise active. Voices can be heard and valued in many ways, including through the use of written surveys, phone calls, personal conversations, or other information gathering. Further, activist parents and educators can advocate for policies at the city level that might assist both schools and families, including issues that affect families such as health care, minimum wage, and transportation, while being especially mindful about equity and inclusion.

In this final chapter, we return to the central themes of the book. Schooling is part of a socialization process. Students do not attend school simply to become employable. Education is cultural work. The deeper goal is to learn to live in a democratic multicultural society on terms of equality. Segregation, inequality, and political divisions in the larger society, as well as within schools themselves, have made this goal more challenging. We challenge the reader to continually ask, what is necessary to become a more egalitarian, effective, and intentional democratic society, and how can schools continue to contribute to that vision?

CONCLUSION

Public schools are supported by the communities in which they are situated because they offer a public good, not just educational credentials so students and families can gain status. One of the central arguments of this book is that schools should not be focused solely on creating or reifying elitism (although we realize that is a significant side effect of what schools do by ranking and grading students). Conferring status and elitism is not a good enough reason for why people without children should fund public schools, or for why all students should be mandated to attend school. Rather, deeper reasons for public education have been made historically, although these arguments have been backgrounded in recent decades. They are, most importantly: (1) We live in a democracy (however imperfect), and the knowledge, skills, and dispositions necessary to effectively participate in shared governance require literacy and education; (2) Child labor laws. Union activists more than a century ago argued persuasively that children should not be working full-time in factories, farms, or other places of employment. The labor movement fought for the rights of children to prepare for their futures, not to be mercilessly exploited for low-wage labor. Therefore, children need a place to go to prepare for their futures while their parents work. These arguments remain persuasive today.

These are two of the most fundamental reasons for investing in public education. There are many more, including becoming reliable citizens, neighbors, parents, taxpayers, and healthy individuals with higher life expectancy. But keeping all of these reasons in mind requires a shift in thinking for many parents, who are, understandably, focused on the personal academic and social success of their own children. The goals of personal academic and financial success and the social goals of becoming good citizens with broader concerns than only oneself do not have to be mutually exclusive. But to prepare for all of these goals, reflection and discussion are needed.

Finally, we want to say that all of the topics in this book—especially intercultural competence—can be understood to be a combination of social-emotional learning and core academic subjects, all of which are priorities for parents and community members, according to surveys. We want to encourage continual dialogue between parents and school personnel to foster mutual support for their many shared goals. We also want to challenge parents and educators to think more deeply and more intentionally about how what they want for their own students fits into what the larger society needs for its schools. Continue looking for ways to achieve high academic standards not only for one's own children but also for all of the children in the school, while also striving to achieve goals like a more inclusive and responsive democracy, meaningful integration, and educational equity.

DISCUSSION QUESTIONS

1. What are the main takeaways of this chapter? What will you remember?
2. What caught your attention in this chapter?
3. Why might it be useful or interesting to learn about other countries' experiences when thinking about schools and about democracy?

4. Did the summary of the book in this chapter fit your understanding of the book?
5. What would you want to know more about after reading this book? What new questions does it raise?
6. How would you wish this book was different?
7. Would you be interested in reading another book about this topic? If so, how might you choose another one?

Recommended Reading for Future Book Studies

Beyond the Bake Sale: The Essential Guide to Family-School Partnerships by Anne T. Henderson, Karen L. Mapp, Vivian R. Johnson, and Don Davies

The Brilliance of Black Boys: Cultivating School Success in the Early Grades by Brian L. Wright with Shelly L. Counsell

City Schools and the American Dream by Pedro Noguera

Cultural Diversity and Education and *Educating Citizens in a Multicultural Society* by James A. Banks

The Death and Life of the Great American School System by Diane Ravitch

Democratic Education by Amy Gutmann

The Dreamkeepers: Successful Teachers of African American Children by Gloria Ladson-Billings

The Essential Conversation: What Parents and Teachers Can Learn From Each Other by Sara Lawrence-Lightfoot

The Flat World and Education: How America's Commitment to Equity Will Determine Our Future by Linda Darling-Hammond

The Inclusion Revolution Is Now: An Innovative Framework for Diversity and Inclusion in the Workplace by Maura G. Robinson

Is Everyone Really Equal? An Introduction to Key Concepts in Social Justice Education by Ozlem Sensoy and Robin DiAngelo

Just Schools: Building Equitable Collaborations with Families and Communities by Ann Ishimaru

The Mind at Work: Valuing the Intelligence of the American Worker by Mike Rose

New Ways to Engage Parents: Strategies and Tools for Teachers and Leaders, K–12 by Patricia A. Edwards

Official Knowledge: Democratic Education in a Conservative Age, Democratic Schools, and *Educating the "Right" Way: Markets, Standards, God, and Inequality* by Michael W. Apple

Parents as Partners in Education: Families and Schools Working Together by Eugenia Hepworth Berger and Mari Riojas-Cortez

The Power of Their Ideas: Lessons for America from a Small School in Harlem and *In Schools We Trust: Creating Communities of Learning in an Era of Testing and Standardization* by Deborah Meier

Savage Inequalities: Children in America's Schools by Jonathan Kozol

School, Family, and Community Partnerships: Your Handbook for Action by Joyce L. Epstein

When Middle-Class Parents Choose Urban Schools: Class, Race, and the Challenge of Equity in Public Education by Linn Posey-Maddox

Why Race and Culture Matter in Schools: Closing the Achievement Gap in America's Classrooms by Tyrone C. Howard

We recommend all books published in the Multicultural Education Book Series with Teachers College Press (James A. Banks, editor).

References

American Library Association. (2022). Voters oppose book bans in libraries. https://www.ala.org/advocacy/voters-oppose-book-bans-libraries

Anyon, J. (2014). *Radical possibilities: Public policy, urban education, and a new social movement* (2nd ed.). Routledge.

Apple, M. W. (2014). *Official Knowledge: Democratic education in a conservative age* (3rd ed.). Routledge.

Banks, J. A. (2003). Series foreword. In M. Dilg (Ed.), *Thriving in the multicultural classroom: Principles and practices for effective teaching* (pp. vii–xi). Teachers College Press.

Banks, J. A. (2007). *Educating citizens in a multicultural society* (2nd ed.). Teachers College Press.

Banks, J. A. (2015). *Cultural diversity and education: Foundations, curriculum, and teaching* (6th ed.). Routledge.

Banks, J. A. (2019). Creating a democratic school in a diverse community. In M. Levinson & J. Fay (Eds.), *Democratic discord in schools: Cases and commentaries in educational ethics* (pp. 39–43). Harvard Education Press.

Berger, E. H., & Riojas-Cortez, M. R. (2016). *Parents as partners in education: Families and schools working together* (9th ed., pp. 32–33). Pearson.

Bonilla-Silva, E. (2013). *Racism without racists: Color-blind racism and the persistence of racial inequality in America* (4th ed.). Rowman-Littlefield.

Bourdieu, P. (1977). *Outline of a theory of practice* (Vol. 16). Cambridge University Press.

Bourdieu, P., & Passeron, J. (1977). *Reproduction in education, society, and culture.* Sage.

Cahill, M. (1999). *Community organizing for school reformers: Train the trainers manual.* Cross City Campaign for Urban School Reform.

Camarota, S. A., Griffith, B., & Zeigler, K. (2023). Mapping the impact of immigration on public schools. Center for Immigration Studies. https://cis.org/Report/Mapping-Impact-Immigration-Public-Schools

Campbell, D. E. (2010). *Choosing democracy: A practical guide to multicultural education* (4th ed.). Pearson.

Carucci, R. (2024, January 24). One more time: Why diversity leads to better team performance. *Forbes*. https://www.forbes.com/sites/roncarucci/2024/01/24/one-more-time-why-diversity-leads-to-better-team-performance/?sh=4fe7478e7c74

Charney, R. S. (2002). *Teaching children to care: Classroom management for ethical and academic growth, K–8* (2nd ed.). Center for Responsive Schools.

Compton-Lilly, C. (2002). *Reading families: The literate lives of urban children*. Teachers College Press.

Cunningham, G. B. (2009). The moderating effect of diversity strategy on the relationship between racial diversity and organizational performance. *Journal of Applied Social Psychology, 39*(6), 1445–1460.

Dahl, R. (2015). *On democracy* (2nd ed.). Yale University Press.

Darling-Hammond, L. (2010). *The flat world and education: How America's commitment to equity will determine our future*. Teachers College Press.

Desmond, M. (2023). *Poverty, by America*. Crown.

DiAngelo, R. (2018) *White fragility: Why it's so hard for White people to talk about racism*. Beacon Press.

Douglass, F. (1852). What to the slave is the 4th of July? National Constitution Center. https://constitutioncenter.org/the-constitution/historic-document-library/detail/frederick-douglass-what-to-the-slave-is-the-fourth-of-july-1852

Edwards, P. (2016). *New ways to engage parents: Strategies and tools for teachers and leaders, K–12*. Teachers College Press.

Epstein, J. L., & Associates. (2009). *School, family, and community partnerships: Your handbook for action* (3rd ed.). Corwin.

Foner, E. (1998). *The story of American freedom*. W. W. Norton.

Frankenberg, E., & Orfield, G. (Eds.). (2007). *Lessons in integration: Realizing the promise of racial diversity in American schools*. University of Virginia Press.

Frankenberg, E., & Orfield, G. (Eds.). (2012). *The resegregation of suburban schools: A hidden crisis in American education*. Harvard Education Press.

Freedom House. (2023). Freedom in the World 2023: Venezuela. https://freedomhouse.org/country/venezuela/freedom-world/2023

Freedom House. (2024). Freedom in the World 2024: Burkina Faso. https://freedomhouse.org/country/burkina-faso/freedom-world/2024

Freire, P., & Macedo, D. (1987). *Literacy: Reading the word and the world*. Bergen & Garvey.

García, O. (2009). *Bilingual education in the 21st century: A global perspective*. Wiley-Blackwell.

Gee, J. P. (2015). *Social linguistics and literacies: Ideology in discourses* (5th ed.). Routledge.

González, N., Moll, L. C., & Amanti, C. (Eds.). (2005). *Funds of knowledge: Theorizing practices in households, communities, and classrooms.* Lawrence Erlbaum.

Gorski, P. C. (2018). *Reaching and teaching students in poverty: Strategies for erasing the opportunity gap* (2nd ed.). Teachers College Press.

Gorski, P., & Swalwell, K. (2023). *Fix injustice, not kids: And other principles for transformative equity leadership*. ASCD.

Gutmann, A. (1999). *Democratic education*. Princeton University Press.

Hawley, W. D. (2007). The social developmental benefits of intergroup contact among children and adolescents. In E. Frankenberg & G. Orfield (Eds.), *Lessons in integration: Realizing the promise of racial diversity in American schools* (pp. 31–56). University of Virginia Press.

Henderson, A. T., Mapp, K. L., Johnson, V. R., & Davies, D. (2007). *Beyond the bake sale: The essential guide to family-school partnerships.* New Press.

Henig, J. R., & Rich, W. C. (Eds.). (2003). *Mayors in the middle: Politics, race, and mayoral control of urban schools.* Princeton University Press.

Himley, M., & Carini, P. (Eds.). (2000). *From another angle: Children's strengths and school standards.* Teachers College Press.

Hlywak, S. (2022, March 24). Large majorities of voters oppose book bans and have confidence in libraries. American Library Association. https://www.ala.org/news/press-releases/2022/03/large-majorities-voters-oppose-book-bans-and-have-confidence-libraries

Ho, P., & Cherng, H. S. (2018). How far can the apple fall? Differences in teacher perceptions of minority and immigrant parents and their impact on academic outcomes. *Social Science Research, 74,* 132–145.

Hofstede, G., Hofstede, G. J., & Minkov, M. (2010). *Cultures and organizations: Software of the mind.* McGraw Hill.

Horowitz, J. M. (2022, October 26). Parents differ sharply by party over what their K-12 children should learn in school. Pew Research Center. https://www.pewresearch.org/social-trends/2022/10/26/parents-differ-sharply-by-party-over-what-their-k-12-children-should-learn-in-school/

Horsford, S. D. (2011). *Learning in a burning house: Educational inequality, ideology and (dis)integration.* Teachers College Press.

Horvat, E. M., Weininger, E. B., & Lareau, A. (2003). From social ties to social capital: Class differences in the relations between schools and parent networks. *American Educational Research Journal, 40*(2), 319–351.

Howard, G. (2016). *We can't teach what we don't know: White teachers, multicultural schools* (3rd ed.). Teachers College Press.

Howard, T. C. (2020). *Why race and culture matter in schools: Closing the achievement gap in America's classrooms* (2nd ed.). Teachers College Press.

Institute for Citizens and Scholars. (2018, October 3). National survey finds just 1 in 3 Americans would pass citizenship test. https://citizensandscholars.org/resource/national-survey-finds-just-1-in-3-americans-would-pass-citizenship-test/

Ishimaru, A. M. (2019). *Just schools: Building equitable collaborations with families and communities.* Teachers College Press.

Jamison, P., Meckler, L., Gordy, P., Morse, C. E., & Alcantara, C. (2023, October 31). Home schooling's rise from fringe to fastest-growing form of education. *The Washington Post.* https://www.washingtonpost.com/education/interactive/2023/homeschooling-growth-data-by-district/

Johnson, R. C., & Nazaryan, A. (2019). *Children of the dream: Why school integration works.* Basic Books.

Kendi, I. X. (2016). *Stamped from the beginning: The definitive history of racist ideas in America.* Nation Books.

Keyssar, A. (2009). *The right to vote: The contested history of democracy in the United States.* Basic Books.

Kids Count Data Center. (2021). Children in poverty in the United States. The Annie E. Casey Foundation. https://datacenter.aecf.org/data/tables/43-children-in-poverty

Kliebard, H. M. (2004). *The struggle for the American curriculum 1893–1958* (3rd ed.). Routledge.

Knoester, M. (2008). Learning to describe, describing to understand. *Schools: Studies in Education, 5*(1), 146–155.

Knoester, M. (2009). Inquiry into urban adolescent independent reading habits: Can Gee's theory of discourses provide insight? *Journal of Adolescent & Adult Literacy, 52*(8), 676–685.

Knoester, M. (2010). Independent reading and the "social turn": How adolescent reading habits and motivation may be related to cultivating social relationships. *Networks, 12*(1), 1–13.

Knoester, M. (2012). *Democratic education in practice: Inside the Mission Hill School.* Teachers College Press.

Knoester, M. (Ed.). (2012). *International struggles for critical democratic education.* Peter Lang.

Knoester, M. (2013). The flat world and books about education reform. *American Journal of Education, 119*(4), 633–639.

Knoester, M., & Au, W. (2017). Standardized testing and school segregation: Like tinder for fire? *Race Ethnicity and Education, 20*(1), 1–14.

Knoester, M., & Gichiru, W. (2021). Inquiry into the educational implications of voting practices of young adults in U.S. mid-term elections. *Journal of Social Studies Research, 45*(4), 267–276.

Knoester, C., & Knoester, M. (2023). Social structure, culture, and the allure of Donald Trump in 2016. *New Political Science, 45*(1), 33–57.

Knoester, M., & Kretz, L. (2017). Why do young adults vote at low rates? Implications for education. *Social Studies Research and Practice, 12*(2), 139–153.

Knoester, M., & Meshulam, A. (2024). *Learning to cross divides: Examining critical multicultural and bilingual schools.* Routledge.

Knoester, M., & Parkison, P. (2015). Where is citizenship education in the age of Common Core State Standards? *Critical Education, 6*(22), 1–16.

Knoester, M., & Parkison, P. (2017). Seeing like a state: How educational policy misreads what is important in schools. *Educational Studies, 53*(3), 247–262.

Knoester, M., & Plikuhn, M. (2015). Influence of siblings on out-of-school reading practices. *Journal of Research in Reading, 39*(4), 469–485.

Knoester, M., & Plikuhn, M. (2016). Inquiry into the independent reading development of first-generation college graduates with advanced degrees. *Journal of Literacy Research, 48*(1), 105–126.

Knoester, M., & Yu, M. (2015). Teachers as cultural workers. In M. E. He, B. D. Schultz, & W. H. Schubert (Eds.), *The Sage guide to curriculum in education* (pp. 190–197). Sage.

Kozol, J. (1992). *Savage inequalities: Children in America's schools.* Harper Perennial.

Ladson-Billings, G. (1995). Toward a theory of culturally relevant pedagogy. *American Educational Research Journal, 32*(3), 465–491.

Ladson-Billings, G. (2014). Culturally relevant pedagogy 2.0: a.k.a. the remix. *Harvard Educational Review, 84*(1), 74–84.

Laguarda, I. (2024, July 26). Swastikas, racial slur found painted at Stamford's AITE high school; local leaders condemn acts. *Stamford Advocate.* https://www.stamfordadvocate.com/local/article/stamford-aite-swastikas-hate-antisemitism-19598839.php

Lake Research Partners. (2023). New polling data finds widespread support for integrating and fully funding public schools. Southern Education Foundation. https://www.brownspromise.org/news/new-polling-data-finds-widespread-support-for-integrating-and-fairly-funding-public-schools

Lareau, A. (2011). *Unequal childhoods: Class, race, and family life* (2nd ed.). University of California Press.

Lareau, A., & Shumar, W. (1996). The problem of individualism in family-school policies. *Sociology of Education,* 69, 24–39.

Lawrence-Lightfoot, S. (2003). *The essential conversation: What parents and teachers can learn from each other.* Ballantine Books.

Lewis, J. (2020, July 30). Together, you can redeem the soul of our nation. *The New York Times.* https://www.nytimes.com/2020/07/30/opinion/john-lewis-civil-rights-america.html

Lipman, P. (2011). *The new political economy of urban education: Neoliberalism, race, and the right to the city.* Routledge.

Logan, J. A., Justice, L. M., Yumus, M., & Chapparo-Moreno, L. J. (2019). When children are not read to at home: The million word gap. *Journal of Developmental and Behavioral Pediatrics, 40*(5), 383–386.

Meier, D. (2002). *In schools we trust: Creating communities of learning in an era of testing and standardization.* Beacon Press.

Meier, D., & Knoester, M. (2017). *Beyond testing: Seven assessments of students and schools more effective than standardized tests.* Teachers College Press.

Meier, D., Sizer, T. R., & Sizer, N. F. (2004). *Keeping school: Letters to families from principals of two small schools.* Beacon Press.

Milner, H. R., Cunningham, H. B., Delale-O'Connor, L., & Kestenberg, E. G. (2019). *"These kids are out of control": Why we must reimagine "classroom management" for equity.* Corwin.

Miner, B. (2013). *Lessons from the heartland: A turbulent half-century of public education in an iconic American city.* New Press.

Muñoz-Pogossian, B., & Winkler, A. (2023, November 27). The persistence of the Venezuelan migrant and refugee crisis. Center for Strategic and International Studies. https://www.csis.org/analysis/persistence-venezuelan-migrant-and-refugee-crisis

Murphy, J., & Torre, D. (2014). *Creating productive cultures in schools: For students, teachers, and parents.* Corwin.

National Literacy Institute. (2025). Literacy Statistics 2024–2025 (Where we are now). https://www.thenationalliteracyinstitute.com/post/literacy-statistics-2024-2025-where-we-are-now

Nichols, S. C. & Berliner, D. C. (2007). *Collateral damage: How high-stakes testing corrupts America's schools.* Harvard Education Press.

Noddings, N. (2013). *Caring: A relational approach to ethics and moral education* (2nd ed.). University of California Press.

Noguera, P. (2003). *City schools and the American dream: Reclaiming the promise of public education.* Teachers College Press.

Oakes, J. (2005). *Keeping track: How schools structure inequality* (2nd ed.). Yale University Press.

Orfield, G., Frankenberg, E., Ee, J., & Ayscue, J. B. (2019, May 10). Harming our common future: America's segregated schools 65 years after Brown. The Civil Rights Project/Proyecto Derechos Civiles.

https://www.civilrightsproject.ucla.edu/research/k-12-education/integration-and-diversity/harming-our-common-future-americas-segregated-schools-65-years-after-brown

Pen America. (2023, April 20). Banned in the USA: State laws supercharge book suppression. https://pen.org/report/banned-in-the-usa-state-laws-supercharge-book-suppression-in-schools/

Posey-Maddox, L. (2014). *When middle-class parents choose urban schools: Class, race and the challenge of equity in public education*. University of Chicago Press.

Rich, M., Cox, A., & Bloch, M. (2016, April 29). Money, race and success: How your school district compares. *The New York Times*. https://www.nytimes.com/interactive/2016/04/29/upshot/money-race-and-success-how-your-school-district-compares.html

Richard, O. C., Murthi, B. P., & Ismail, K. (2007). The impact of racial diversity on intermediate and long-term performance: The moderating role of environmental context. *Strategic Management Journal, 28*(12), 1213–1233.

Rothstein, R. (2017). *The color of law: A forgotten history of how our government segregated America*. W. W. Norton.

Rowe, M. P. (1990). Barriers to equality: The power of subtle discrimination to maintain unequal opportunity. *Employee Responsibilities and Rights Journal, 3*, 153–163.

Sahlberg, P. (2021). *Finnish lessons, 3.0: What can the world learn from educational change in Finland?* Teachers College Press.

Sensoy, O., & DiAngelo, R. (2017). *Is everyone really equal? An introduction to key concepts in social justice education* (2nd ed.). Teachers College Press.

Schaeffer, K. (2021, December 10). America's public school teachers are far less racially and ethnically diverse than their students. Pew Research Center. https://www.pewresearch.org/short-reads/2021/12/10/americas-public-school-teachers-are-far-less-racially-and-ethnically-diverse-than-their-students/

Schaeffer, K. (2024, June 6). U.S. public, private and charter schools in 5 charts. Pew Research Center. https://www.pewresearch.org/short-reads/2024/06/06/us-public-private-and-charter-schools-in-5-charts/

Siegel, D. J., & Bryson, T. P. (2016). *No drama discipline: The whole-brain way to calm the chaos and nurture your child's developing mind*. Bantam.

Somé, T. H., & Orelus, P. W. (Eds.). (2015). *Immigration and schooling: Redefining the 21st century America*. Information Age.

Southern Poverty Law Center (2024). Hate and extremism. https://www.splcenter.org/issues/hate-and-extremism

Streib, L. Y. (2010). *Inviting families into the classroom: Learning from a life in teaching*. Teachers College Press.

Valencia, R. R. (Ed.). (1997). *The evolution of deficit thinking: Educational thought and practice.* Falmer Press.

Walker, V. S. (2000). Valued segregated schools for African American children in the South, 1935–1969: A review of common themes and characteristics. *Review of Educational Research, 70*(3), 253–285.

Ward, L. M., & Bridgewater, E. (2023). Media use and the development of racial attitudes among U.S. youth. *Child Development Perspectives, 17*(2), 83–89.

Wright, B. L., & Counsell, S. L. (2018). *The brilliance of Black boys: Cultivating school success in the early grades.* Teachers College Press.

Wright, P. W., Wright, P. D., & O'Connor, S. W. (2015). *All about IEPs: Answers to frequently asked questions about IEPs.* Harbor House Law Press.

Zajacova, A., & Lawrence, E. M. (2018, April 1). The relationship between education and health: Reducing disparities through a contextual approach. *Annual Review of Public Health, 39*(1), 273–289.

Zehr, M. A. (2001, March 21). Out of Africa. *Education Week.* https://www.edweek.org/leadership/out-of-africa/2001/03

Zimmer, A., & Mediratta, K. (2004). *Lessons from the field of school reform organizing.* Odonian Press.

Zippia (2024). Teacher demographics and statistics in the US. https://www.zippia.com/teacher-jobs/demographics/

Index

About the Authors

Matthew Knoester is a professor and chair of the Educational Studies Department at Ripon College. He received his PhD in curriculum and instruction from the University of Wisconsin–Madison. He is a former National Board–certified teacher, teaching primarily in the Boston Public Schools. His research analyzes teaching practices and focuses on literacy development, family engagement, education for democratic citizenship, equity and anti-racism, bilingualism, and authentic assessments. Three of his books have received the Critics' Choice Book Award from the American Educational Studies Association.

Maura G. Robinson is an intercultural development administrator and award-winning CEO with 30 years of corporate experience. She is a leading authority on cultural competency management. Maura has facilitated hundreds of workshops and seminars around the country and internationally. She has worked with over 300 clients, including those in profit and nonprofit settings, such as school districts, the automobile industry, the power and electric service industry, hospitality, banking, and religious settings.

Touorizou Herve Somé is an associate professor at Ripon College. As a Fulbright Scholar, he earned his PhD in 2007 in the Social Foundations program at the University of Buffalo. He has published many articles and peer-reviewed book chapters relating to education reform in the United States and higher education finance in Africa. His research interests include globalization, neoliberalism, multiculturalism, and higher education finance in Africa. He is a public scholar who actively took part in the people's movement for democracy in Burkina Faso, leading to the ousting of President Compaoré.